RICHARD JORDAN GATLING'S GUN PATENTS

This book is a compilation of the gun patents of Richard Jordan Gatling, who is considered the father of repeating weapons, and whose inventions had a great impact on the history of the United States and the military history of many other countries.

All documents shown here are reproductions of the original patents, wich have been digitally enhanced to achieve higher image quality.

The author gives general permission to copy and distribute any patents and patent drawings or parts thereof in any medium, in any manner whatsoever without further attribution or notice to the author. All other rights reserved.

Neither the author nor the publilsher assumes any responsibility for the use, misure or the accuracy of the information contained in this publication.

CONTENTS

Biography of Richard Jordan Gatling ……………..……………………………... 5

Ancient photos of Gatling gun ……………………………………..…...………... 7

Patent No. 36836 / R.J.Gatling / November 4, 1862 …………………….…..…… 15

Patent No. 47631 / R.J.Gatling / May 9, 1865 …………………........…..……… 19

Patent No. 112138 / R.J.Gatling / February 28, 1871 …………………………… 27

Patent No. 125563 / R.J.Gatling / April 9, 1872 …………...……………….…… 37

Patent No. 145563 / R.J.Gatling / December 16, 1873 ……....……………..…… 45

Patent No. 497781 / R.J.Gatling / May 23, 1893 ………...…………………….… 51

Patent No. 499534 / R.J.Gatling / June 13, 1893 …………………………….…... 61

Patent No. 502185 / R.J.Gatling / July 25, 1893 ………...……………….…..….. 67

Patent No. 502882 / R.J.Gatling / August 8, 1893 ……………………….……… 75

Patent No. 504831 / R.J.Gatling / September 12, 1893 …………………….…….. 79

Biography of Richard Jordan Gatling

Richard Jordan Gatling was born in Hertford County, North Carolina in 1818 and he was a son of a farmer. At the age of 21, Gatling created a screw propeller for steamboats, without realizing that one had been patented just months beforehand by John Ericsson. While living in North Carolina, he worked in the county clerk's office, taught school briefly, and became a merchant. At the age of 36, Gatling moved to St. Louis, Missouri, where he worked in a dry goods store and invented a rice-sowing machine and a wheat drill. After an attack of smallpox, Gatling became interested in medicine. He graduated from the Ohio Medical College in 1850 with an MD. Although he had his MD, he never practiced; he was more interested in a career as an inventor.

By the early 1850s, Gatling was successful enough in business to offer marriage to Jemima Sanders, 19 years younger than Gatling and the daughter of a prominent Indianapolis physician. They married on October 25, 1854. Her younger sister Zerelda was married to David Wallace, the governor of Indiana.

Gatling invented the Gatling gun after he noticed that a majority of the soldiers fighting in the Civil War were lost to disease rather than gunshots. A working prototype was developed in 1861. In 1862, he founded the Gatling Gun Company in Indianapolis, Indiana to market the gun. The first six production guns were destroyed during a fire in December 1862 at the factory. All six of them had been manufactured at Gatling's expense. Undaunted, Gatling arranged for another thirteen to be manufactured at the Cincinnati Type Factory. Although the gun was developed during the Civil War, it saw very little action. This is partly because Gatling was accused of being a copperhead because of his North Carolina roots, but this was never proven. Gatling was never affiliated with the Confederate States government or military, nor did he live in the South during the Civil War.

General Benjamin F. Butler bought 12 and Admiral David Dixon Porter bought one, it was not until 1866 that the US Government officially purchased Gatling guns. In 1870, he sold his patents for the Gatling gun to Colt. Gatling remained president of the Gatling Gun Company until it was fully absorbed by Colt in 1897.

In 1893, Gatling patented a Gatling gun that replaced the hand cranked mechanism with an electric motor, a relatively new invention at the time, achieving a rate of fire of 3,000 rounds per minute. The hand-cranked Gatling gun was declared obsolete by the United States Army in 1911.

Decades later, the mechanical concept was resurrected and wedded to electrically-driven cranking in the M61 Vulcan. That cannon has given rise to numerous variations scaled up to as high as 37 mm and down to 5.56 mm calibers offering versions that are gas-operated as well.

Later in his life, Gatling patented inventions to improve toilets, bicycles, steam-cleaning of raw wool, pneumatic power, and many other fields. He was elected as the first president of the American Association of Inventors and Manufacturers in 1891, serving for six years.

In his final years, Gatling moved back to St. Louis, Missouri, to form a new company for manufacturing his steam plows, or tractors. While in New York City to visit his daughter and to talk with his patent agency, Gatling died at his daughter's home on February 26, 1903. He is interred at the Crown Hill Cemetery in Indianapolis, Indiana.

His contributions were commemorated by the U.S. Navy during World War II when the Fletcher Class Destroyer DD-671 was christened the USS Gatling.

Ancient photos of Gatling gun

Gatling gun model 1893 with ten .31-inch octagon barrels

Rapid fire .58 Gatling gun mounted on light field artillery carriage

A battery of 1-inch Gatling guns in Dakota Territory, c.1877

Officers of the US Marine Corps with two Gatling guns, c.1896

American soldiers with mobile Gatling gun, c.1899

Gatling gun with a Bruce Feed near Manilla c.1899, with two men preparing 20-round wooden loading blocks

Men of the US Infantry Gatling Gun detachment in the Forbidden City, Beijing c.1900

American Gatling guns during the Spanish American War of 1898

A five barrel 1877 Model 'Bulldog' Gatling gun with a Bruce feed, Philippines c.1899

Gatling gun in Manilla c.1899

A British Gatling Gun detachment using Broadwell Drums, South Africa c.1879

A British Gatling Gun detachment using Broadwell Drums, South Africa c.1879

Gatling gun in Philippines, c.1895

Dr Richard Gatling with a Colt 'Bulldog' Gatling Model 1893

Gunner Charles Goodrich c.1879

A man with a Gatling gun aboard the USS Indiana, c.1895

UNITED STATES PATENT OFFICE.

RICHARD J. GATLING, OF INDIANAPOLIS, INDIANA.

IMPROVEMENT IN REVOLVING BATTERY-GUNS.

Specification forming part of Letters Patent No. **36,836**, dated November 4, 1862.

To all whom it may concern:

Be it known that I, RICHARD J. GATLING, of Indianapolis, county of Marion, and State of Indiana, have invented new and useful Improvements in Fire-Arms; and I do hereby declare that the following is a full and exact description thereof, reference being had to the accompanying drawings, making part of this specification, in which—

Figure 1 is a side elevation of the gun with the upper portion of the wheels cut away. Fig. 2 is a vertical longitudinal section through the center of the gun. Fig. 3 is a top view of the gun with the top half of the external casing, A, left off and the middle portion of the barrels cut away to shorten the drawing. Fig. 4 is a transverse section through lock-cylinder on line $x\,y$ in Figs. 1 and 2. Fig. 5 is an end view of the grooved carrier C which receives the cartridges or cartridge-chambers. Fig. 6 is a side view of one of the tubes containing the mainspring and hammer of one of the locks. Fig. 7 is a perspective view of the ring P which surrounds the forward end of the lock-cylinder D, having inclined planes on its rear edge for cocking and drawing back the hammers to their proper position.

The object of this invention is to obtain a simple, compact, durable, and efficient fire-arm for war purposes, to be used either in attack or defence, one that is light when compared with ordinary field-artillery, that is easily transported, that may be rapidly fired, and that can be operated by few men.

The invention consists in a singularly-constructed revolving lock cylinder or breech, in combination with a grooved carrier and barrels all rigidly fixed upon the same shaft, and all of which revolve together when the gun is in operation, the locks and grooves in the carrier and the barrels all being parallel with the axis of revolution.

The invention also consists in the novel means employed in cocking and firing the gun without the use of a trigger by means of the inclined plane on the rear edge of the ring P, which surrounds the forward end of the lock-cylinder, and also in the novel use of the inner tubes (which contain the locks) to press the cartridge-chambers firmly against the rear ends of the barrels while being discharged, and

in the outer casing and disk, which protects the locks from injury.

Similar letters of reference indicate corresponding parts in the several figures.

To enable others skilled in the art to make and use my invention, I will proceed to describe its construction and operation.

I construct my gun usually with six ordinary rifle-barrels, E, fixed at their rear and forward ends into circular plates F and G, which are rigidly secured to a shaft, N, upon which is also rigidly fixed the grooved carrier C and lock-cylinder D and cog-wheel K. A case or shield, A, covers and protects the lock-cylinder and cog-wheel. All of these several parts are mounted on a frame, B, and are supported by an ordinary gun-carriage. The lock-cylinder D is perforated longitudinally with six holes, (corresponding to the number of barrels,) as shown in Fig. 4, and has slots cut through from the surface of the cylinder to the holes to admit the projecting portion of the hammers b. In the perforations or holes in the lock-cylinder the locks (one of which is shown in elevation in Fig. 6) are placed.

The locks are constructed of the tubes $a\,a$, &c., having a flanged breech-pin, c, secured in their rear ends and provided with hammers b and mainsprings d, all formed and arranged as clearly shown in section in Fig. 2.

C is a grooved carrier for conveying the cartridge-chambers from the reservoir or hopper H up to the position in which they are fired, and thence on around until they fall out by their own weight; but that the cartridge-chambers may be removed with certainty from the grooved carrier C a comb or rake is provided and attached to the frame, as shown by the red lines in Figs. 2 and 3.

P, Figs. 2, 3, and 7, is a ring encircling the forward end of the lock-cylinder D, and is rigidly secured by lugs to the frame B. The rear edge of this ring is formed into two inclined planes, as clearly shown in Fig. 3, the greater inclined plane serving to push back or cock the hammers b as they are successively revolved, while the lesser inclined plane serves to push the hammers back into their proper places within the tubes a after they have struck the percussion-cap, so as to allow the cartridge-chambers to drop from the carrier.

The disk I forms a division in the case A, the forward portion of the case forming a shield or covering for the locks, while the rear division contains and protects the cog-wheel K and L. In the forward face of the disk I a small steel plug, O, is inserted, having its forward face rounded or swelled out slightly beyond the face of the disk. This swell is for the purpose of pressing the tubes *a* forward against the cartridge-chambers R, and thus pressing the cartridge-chambers firmly against the rear end of the barrel at the time of each and every discharge, thereby preventing the escape of gas from the ignited powder. The forward motion of the tubes *a*, caused by the swell O on disk I, also assists in compressing the mainsprings *d*, thereby increasing the force of the blow from the lock-hammers *b* upon the percussion-caps on the nipples of the cartridge-chambers.

The rounded heads of the breech-pin *c* bear against the forward face of the disk I, being kept in their position by the coiled springs *e e*, &c., which surround the rear ends of the tubes *a a*, &c., the springs *e* bearing against the rear end of the lock-cylinder and against the flange of the breech-pin *c*. By this arrangement the forward ends of the locks are kept flush with the forward face of the lock-cylinder until they are revolved opposite the swell *o*, when they are pressed forward, as before described.

The shaft N, upon which the lock-cylinder D, carrier C, barrels E, and cog-wheel K are rigidly secured, has a bearing near its rear end in disk I and a bearing at its forward end in a box on the frame B. A crank-shaft, M, runs through the rear part of case A and has fixed upon it the small cog-wheel or pinion L and crank S.

An adjusting-screw, T, is placed in the box opposite the forward end of shaft N, for regulating the pressure upon the cartridge-chambers R. The cartridge-chambers R, (any desired number of which may be used,) being loaded, are placed in the hopper or reservoir, with their nipple or cap ends toward the hammers, over the grooved carriers C, when, by rotating the crank S, which carries with it the shaft M, and pinion L, which meshes into the large cog-wheel K, thereby revolving the shaft N, lock-cylinder D, carrier C, and barrels E, the cartridges drop or rather roll into the grooves of carrier C and are carried by it up to the position in which they are discharged. The hammers, cartridge-chambers, and barrels all being on a line parallel to the axis of revolution, it is impossible for the cartridges to be out of place when discharged.

The hammers *b* are pushed back by the large inclined plane on the rear edge of the ring P, and when they have passed the highest point of the inclined plane they are driven forward against the percussion-cap on the nipple of the cartridge-chamber by the coiled mainspring *e* with sufficient force to explode the cap and discharge the cartridge, after which the cartridge-holder is carried on around until it drops out of the carrier by its own weight, when it is ready to be taken up and reloaded.

I do not claim the use of the grooved or fluted revolving carrier C, separately considered, and when the same is made to revolve separately and independently of the barrels and breech, the same being an old device; neither do I claim the direct combination thereof with an automatic revolving gear or with a device for pressing the cartridge-chamber against the barrel when used alone for that purpose; but

What I do claim as new and as my invention, and desire to secure by Letters Patent, is—

1. The combination of the lock-cylinder or breech D with the grooved carrier C, circular plate F, and barrels E E, &c., the lock-cylinder or breech, carrier, and circular plate being firmly fastened upon the main shaft N, and the locks, grooves in the carrier, and barrels being arranged on a line parallel with the axis of revolution, the whole revolving together when the gun is in operation, substantially as described.

2. In the construction of revolving fire-arms, the use of as many locks as there are barrels, said locks revolving simultaneously with the breech and barrels, and being arranged and operated substantially as set forth.

3. The stationary ring P, provided with inclined planes on its rear edge, in combination with lock-cylinder D and locks, when constructed and operated for the purposes substantially as set forth.

4. The tubes *a a*, &c., furnished with the flanged breech-pins *c c*, &c., and springs *e e*, &c., and which contain the lock-hammers *b b*, &c., and mainsprings *d d*, &c., in combination with the revolving breech D, disk I, and swell *o*, when constructed, arranged, and operated for the purposes substantially as set forth.

5. The disk I, in combination with the external breech-piece or casing, A, which forms a shield or covering for the lock-cylinder and which protects the locks and cog-wheels from injury.

RICHARD J. GATLING.

Witnesses:
  A. F. MAYHEW,
  W. O. ROCKWOOD.

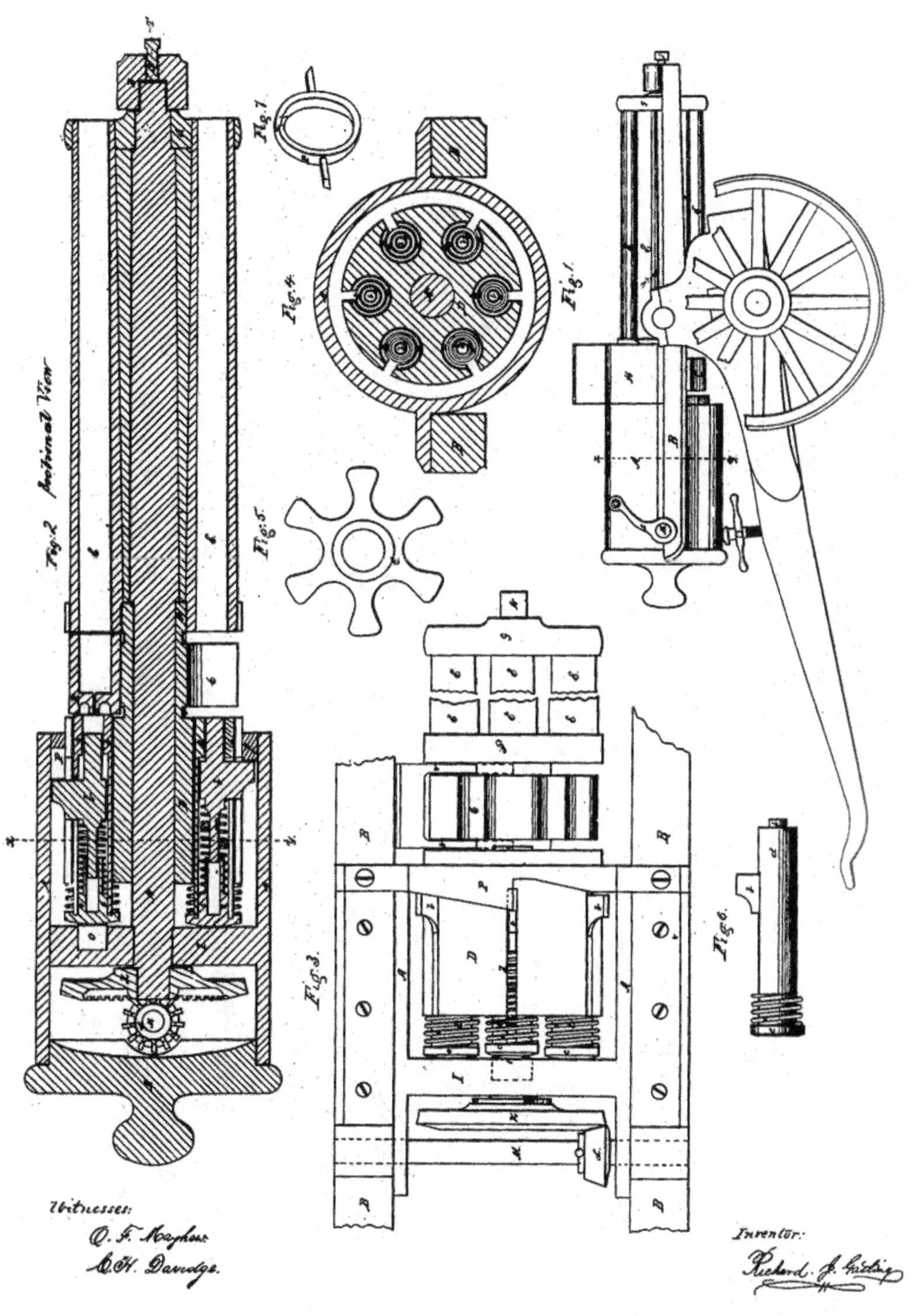

R. J. Gatling
Machine Gun.
Nº 36,836.   Patented Nov. 4, 1862
Fig.1
Fig.4
Fig.5.
Fig.2 Sectional View
Fig.3.
Fig.5.
Fig.6.
Witnesses:
Inventor:
Richard J. Gatling

UNITED STATES PATENT OFFICE.

RICHARD J. GATLING, OF INDIANAPOLIS, INDIANA.

IMPROVEMENT IN BATTERY-GUNS.

Specification forming part of Letters Patent No. **47,631**, dated May 9, 1865.

To all whom it may concern:

Be it known that I, RICHARD JORDAN GATLING, of Indianapolis, county of Marion and State of Indiana, have made certain new and useful Improvements in Fire Arms, which I term a "Battery-Gun;" and I do hereby declare the following to be a full, clear, and exact description of the same, reference being had to the annexed drawings, making part of this specification, in which—

Figure 1 is a side elevation of the gun with its carriage and wheels. Fig. 2 is a plan of the same, or the mounted gun as viewed from above. Fig. 3 is a partial axial section on a horizontal plane, showing parts of the mechanism in plan. It is taken on the line $x\,x$, Fig. 14. Fig. 4 is a vertical longitudinal axial section, the locks and main shaft being shown in elevation. It is taken in the line $y\,y$, Fig. 14. Fig. 5 is a perspective view of the ring furnished with inclined planes set spirally in relation to the axis of the gun and used for giving the longitudinal motions to the locks and breech-pins. Fig. 6 is a perspective view of the cocking-ring, which is used for drawing the lock-hammers back and liberating them to explode the cartridges when the gun is being operated. Fig. 7 is a transverse vertical section, at right angles to the axis of the gun, on the line $x\,x$, Fig. 3. Fig. 8 is an end view of the cylinder within which the locks are inclosed, and showing the perforations in the heads of the said cylinder, which form guides for the locks. Fig. 9 is an elevation of said cylinder. Fig. 10 is a longitudinal sectional view of one of the cartridge-boxes, from which the cartridges are fed into the gun, and is a section on line $x\,x$, Fig. 11, and shows the cartridges in place. Fig. 11 is a top view of the cartridge-box. Fig. 12 is an elevation of one of the locks. Fig. 13 is a longitudinal central section of one of the locks on the line $z\,z$, Fig. 12. Fig. 14 is a rear view of the gun with the cascabel and screw-cap, which closes the end of the chamber occupied by the rotating gears, removed. Figs. 15, 16 are views of the cap which is used to close a cavity in the cartridge-carrier when temporarily disused.

Similar letters of reference indicate corresponding parts in the several figures.

The main characteristic of my invention is a gun having a series of barrels with a carrier and lock-cylinder rigidly fastened to the main shaft and rotating simultaneously and continuously under the rotation of suitable gearing, the cartridges being fed into the cavities of the carrier, driven endwise into the barrels, then exploded, and the empty cartridge-cases withdrawn without any pause in the operation.

I will now proceed to describe in detail the peculiarities, the construction, and the operation of my invention.

The nature of my invention consists, first, in attaching the lock-cylinder in which the locks reciprocate longitudinally, the carrier in whose cavities the cartridges are deposited consecutively and the barrels rigidly to a revolving shaft, so that each lock shall at all times be in line with the cartridge-cavity in the carrier and with the barrel to which it appertains, and so that the operations of loading, firing, and extracting of the spent cartridge-cases may proceed under the impulse of the driving mechanism continuously, each barrel, cartridge-cavity, and lock forming a gun in itself, which in the course of its rotation is brought into contact with the requisite relational devices for manipulating and operating it and causing the various parts to perform their appropriate functions of receiving the cartridge from the feeder, thrusting it directly into the bore of the gun, cocking the hammer, exploding the cartridge, and finally extracting the spent cartridge-case, all of which several operations are effected without stopping the rotation of the barrels, locks, &c., when the gun is being operated; secondly, in the construction of the locks, each of which consists of a breech-pin united to a butt-piece and having a sleeve and lug moving upon it, which, under the impulse of a spring, acts as a hammer to drive the igniting-punch against the flange of the cartridge, the lock also affording attachment for the hook which slips over the flange of the cartridge and on the rearward motion of the lock withdraws the spent cartridge-case; thirdly, in the camring which occupies a position at the rear of the lock-cylinder, and has within it two spiral or cam shaped faces, one of them operating upon the butt-end of the lock mechanisms in each case to drive the cartridge from the cavity in the carrier into the bore of the gun, and the other cam-face to act upon a lug on the said lock mechanism to withdraw the breech-pin, bringing with it the spent shell or case and retreating so far as to open the cavity in the carrier for the deposition of another cartridge; fourthly, in the cap or plug which is adapted to be laid over any such one of the cavities in the carrier as it may be desired shall not receive the cartridge, owing to some disarrangement of the parts or the bursting of the barrel, which may render that section of the gun inoperative.

The gun, speaking of it in general terms, is mounted upon its carriage, consisting of the wheels B B and the trail C, and is secured thereon by the usual cap, D, over the trunnions F, which project laterally from the frame H, by which the gun is supported and within which it revolves. The breech is raised and lowered by the elevating-screw E. The revolving portion, consisting of the lock-cylinder carrying the loading and firing mechanism, the cartridge-carrier, and the barrels, is attached to and supported by an axial or main shaft, N, whose forward end is journaled in the end piece of the frame H, and the rear end in a diaphragm or partition, I, within the casing J, which is supported by flanges on the frame H. The rotation of this shaft and the devices recited above, which are rigidly attached thereto, is accomplished by means of a hand-crank, K, whose shaft L carries a bevel-pinion, M, which gears into a bevel-wheel on the shaft N. (Shown clearly in Fig. 14.) The gearing is located in a chamber occupying the rear of the casing J, whose end is closed by a screw-cap, O, with an attached cascabel.

It has been stated that the cylinder P, which carries the loading and firing mechanism, the cartridge-carrier Q, and the barrels R are attached to the axial shaft N by a feather fitting into them and a groove in the shaft N, so as to revolve with it. The barrels are secured thereon by means of two disks or heads, S S', which are fast on the shaft and in which they are secured, the rear disk, S', being clamped between the sleeve T and the carrier Q, to be hereinafter described. The barrels R are secured in the said disks in any suitable way, and are shown as secured into the rear disk and passing through the forward disk, being fitted thereon, so as to be sufficiently tight to hold the contents of the casing U, which surrounds the barrels and holds water, plaster-of-paris, or other material to preserve the barrels from injurious expansion by excessive heating. The said fluid is inserted and withdrawn through the orifice U', other provision, not necessary to describe, being made for more solid contents, should it be required.

The cartridge-carrier Q is fitted between the disk S and the cylinder P, and has a number of grooves in its periphery which are parallel with the axis of revolution, are in line with and agree in number with the barrels, which may be of any desired number. I have shown in my drawings but four, but the invention has no reference to specific number. These grooves are shown very clearly in Fig. 7, and are adapted as the carrier passes under the box containing the cartridges to receive each of them a cartridge to be thrust into the bore of the gun by the suitable mechanism, which will be described in detail presently, when the action will be more properly treated of under that general head of this specification which is devoted to describing the operation.

Immediately in the rear of the cartridge-carrier Q is a cylindrical chamber, P, likewise attached by feather or other suitable device to the axial-shaft N, and supported at the rear by the nut V, which screws upon the threaded portion of the shaft N. This cylinder is shown by a rear end elevation in Fig. 8 and side elevation at Fig. 9, as well as being shown in its place by the two longitudinal general sections, Figs. 3 and 4; but as it is a mere shell with longitudinal slots in its periphery and orifices in each end, the purpose of which slots and orifices will be presently explained, the sections, Figs. 3 and 4, only show the detached parts which are cut by the section, and do not give so correct an impression of its form and character as Figs. 8 and 9.

In the rear immediate neighborhood of the cylinder P, but not in connection therewith, is a cam-ring, W. (Shown in perspective in Fig. 5, and also in its place in the sections Figs. 3 and 4.) This cam-ring W abuts at its rear upon and is bolted to the diaphragm I, which is a part of and a partition in the stationary casing J. The exterior cylindrical portion of this stationary ring is embraced by the casing J, and the inside is provided with two cam-surfaces, W' W'', which alternately advance and retract the loading mechanism, which will be presently described, and in connection therewith I shall take occasion to describe more explicitly the action of these cams to which I now merely refer.

Around the anterior portion of the cylinder P is another stationary ring, X, which I call the "cocking-ring," Fig. 6, whose forward edge is in the plane of revolution of the barrels, but its rear edge forms a spiral or cam surface, which impinges upon a lug on the lock-hammer, and withdraws it toward the rear until it reaches the end of the incline plane or cam-surface X', when it drops off, and is thereby suddenly released to the influence of the spring and caused to strike the collar attached to the igniting-punch, as will be more fully explained in the next paragraph, which will explain in detail the construction of the moving parts, which load and explode the cartridge and withdraw the spent capsule or case.

The loading, firing, and cartridge-case-extracting device is shown in its place in Figs. 3 and 4, and is more particularly exhibited on a larger scale in Figs. 12 and 13, in the former of which it is shown in elevation and in the latter in section. It consists of a butt-piece, a, with lugs a' a'', and united to the breech-pin b by the rounded shank b' of the latter, which forms a mandrel for the traversing of the sleeve c of the hammer, which has a longitudinal reciprocating motion upon it, and has a lug, c', for a purpose to be explained. d is a collar and punch, the former of which slides upon the mandrel c, and the latter—the punch—slides in a slot in the breech-pin b. e is the retractor, with a hook, e', at its end, which slips over the flange of the cartridge as the breech-pin b drives the cartridge into the bore of the gun. The shank of the retractor is pinned to the breech-pin, and the butt of the retractor is also dovetailed into the collar f, which is a part of or fastened to the breech-pin b. d' is a spiral spring, which abuts against the forward end of the butt-piece a and against the shoulder of the sleeve-hammer c, so as to simultaneously act upon each of these faces. To avoid prolixity I shall defer an explanation of the various offices performed by the devices recited in this paragraph to that section of this specification which treats of the operation of the gun, as it naturally calls for lucid and consecutive statement in that place, and I desire to avoid needless repetition.

Figs. 10 and 11 show the cartridge-box into which the cartridges are packed for transportation, and out of which they are fed by their own gravity, one by one, into the cavities of the carrier Q as it revolves beneath them. These boxes are rectangular sheet-metal cases, adapted to the size of the cartridge, which, it is hardly necessary to say, are adapted to the bore of the gun. The sectional view, Fig. 10, shows the appearance of the cartridges Z in the case Y, and Y' shows the cap by which they are retained in the case during transportation. These views, Figs. 10 and 11, are on a larger scale than the view Fig. 7, but the latter gives the best view of the position of the cartridge-box Y as it is in place, viewed from the rear, showing a section on the line x x, Fig. 3, except that the flanged ends of the cartridges are shown.

The rest or holder A, which forms a cap over the cartridge-carrier Q, and retains the cartridges in their cavities until they are projected into the bore of the gun, is hinged to an elbow-piece, A', which is suitably fastened by bolts to the frame H of the gun. This holder, which is shown most effectively in Fig. 2, has an inclined ledge, in which the box of cartridges fits, so as to allow them to pass out consecutively into the cavities of the carrier. The slot in the cap of the rest allows them to be seen as they pass, while the curved under side of the cap retains them in their places.

The usual sights, B' B'', are placed over the breech and muzzle of the gun, and need no particular description, as they do not differ from those in ordinary use.

Fixed metallic cartridges are used in this gun, and are contained in cases, of which a number are kept on hand and refilled as occasion may require.

Metallic caps or covers, Figs. 15, 16, may be placed over such one or more of the cavities in the carrier as may be rendered necessary by the temporary disablement of the barrel or lock mechanism appertaining to the said cavity. This has the effect of shutting off the feed of the cartridges into one or more of the barrels which are incapacitated for service, and admits of the use of the remaining barrels without cessation other than to fit the cap over that cartridge-cavity withdrawn from service.

The gun can be so constructed as to revolve to the right or left or back and forth, as may be desired. This modification can be effected by adding to or changing the spiral cam-faces W' W'' and stationary cocking-ring X, so as to produce such results.

The operation of my gun is as follows: The gun, being mounted on the carriage or on a rotary platform or turn-table in such a manner as may best suit the purpose of defense or offense for which it is designed, is trained and sighted, and an attendant deposits a box of cartridges, with the uncovered end downward, upon the inclined ledge of the holder A. The gunner then seizes the handle of the crank K and revolves the pinion M, which rotates with it the axial or main shaft N.

While desiring to avoid repetition I must here repeat that the cylinder which contains the loading, cocking, and firing mechanism is fast to the shaft, as are also the cartridge-carriers Q and the barrels R, the latter through the intervention of the disks S S', into which the rear and forward ends, respectively, of the barrels are secured. I will now trace the consecutive motions and show the action of the various parts by which one cartridge is rammed to its place, exploded, and the empty shell retracted, and this will serve as a full description when it is stated that each barrel and its attendant devices are a complete gun in themselves and the series is but a repetition in duplicate, triplicate, or quadruplicate, as the case may be, of the operation of a single gun, this multiplication of parts constituting a compound gun with a number only limited by the question of convenience and utility, the specific number being indeterminate and not included within the scope of my claims.

To resume. The shaft and attendant machinery being revolved by the gearing, one of the hollows in the cartridge-carrier Q, passing under the open end of the cartridge-box, receives a cartridge and carries it over, the loading and firing plunger (Fig. 12) revolving with it until the rear end of the butt-piece a comes in contact with and commences to ascend the inclined plane or cam-face W' of the stationary ring W. As it ascends this inclined plane the breech-pin b is moved forward, thrusting the cartridge into the barrel, while the direct longitudinal motion of the loader is secured by the traversing of the lug a'' in the longitudinal slot of the cylinder P, Fig. 9. As the plunger moves forward it carries the sleeve-hammer c with it until the lug c' on the hammer comes in contact with the rear or cam face of the stationary cocking-ring X, Fig. 6. By means of this ring the hammer is drawn toward the rear, compressing the spring d', which in no wise interferes with the action of the plunger, which continues its forward motion until the rear of the butt-piece a arrives on the flat portion of the came-face W′ to a point marked with a red star in Fig. 5, which indicates the firing-point, and is at or near the lowest point reached by the barrel in its rotation on the central axis. This endwise motion of the plunger has brought the forward end of the breech-piece close against the flange of the cartridge, which is firmly held in the chambered recess at the rear of the barrel, the exploding-punch, whose point protrudes a little beyond the end of the breech-pin, being forced back even with the same by the pressure upon the flange of the cartridge. This leaves a small space between the collar d of the punch and the flange f of the breech-pin, as may be seen in the lower one of the two flanges as represented in Fig. 4.

It is proper to mention at this point that at some period of the contact of the breech-pin b with the rear end of the cartridge the hook $e′$ is slipped over the flange, and when the cartridge is rammed home occupies a recess in the edge of the bore.

To proceed with the description of the motion, after this apparent digression, in which the status of the different parts at the point of firing has been considered, we shall find that the lug $e′$ of the hammer has been withdrawn rearwardly to the end of the cam on the cocking-ring X X′, Fig. 6, when by the continued revolution it is freed to the action of the spring $d′$, and the hammer c forcibly driven against the collar d of the exploding-punch, closing the space between d and f, and causing the point of the punch to indent the flange of the cartridge, which contains the fulminate, and explodes the charge. The two surfaces which come together with force in this percussive action consist of the annular collar and the flange of the breech-pin, and their extended surfaces receiving the blow are a safeguard against injury by battering or upsetting. The flat portion which terminates the came-face W′ is intended to hold the breech-piece firmly against the rear of the cartridge for a short space of time as a precaution in case of a cartridge hanging fire, and it will be observed that the rearward force of the discharge is received upon the end of the breech-pin and butt-piece, which I have called occasionally a "plunger" for the sake of convenience, and this is supported in the rear by the cam-surface of the ring W, which is firmly secured in the diaphragm I and casing J.

The plunger is of a determinate adjusted length, and occupies the whole space, when fired, between the flat portion of the cam-surface W and the rear of the barrel. The load having been discharged, the rear of the butt-piece, under the continued rotation, passes beyond the surface W′, and the lug $a′$ is engaged by the pointed end of the cam-surface W″, which is also inside of the ring W. This incline has the effect of withdrawing the plunger, which in turn, by the engagement of the hook $e′$ with the flange of the cartridge-case or spent capsule, retracts the latter from the bore and allows it to drop out of the cavity of the carrier Q toward the ground.

At the risk of tedius repetition I would here repeat that while the reciprocating motions of the parts are of course intermittent, as there are periods during which they pause for a fraction of a second, and cannot be strictly considered as incessant, yet the revolving motion of the barrels and attendant mechanism is absolutely continuous while the guns pass through the various stages of loading, firing, or retracting cartridge-cases and withdrawing the plunger to make room for another cartridge to occupy the groove in the carrier, thus bringing the succession of guns to the loading and firing points, and causing them to follow each other in a constantly-recurring cycle of operations, all the balls being discharged at one point and following in the wake of each other with precision unless by the training of the gun in a horizontal or other plane the sheet of balls is made to sweep a section of the circle within its range.

The gun described, which has four barrels, can be discharged at the rate of two hundred shots per minute, and guns on the same principle with a larger number of barrels can be made to discharge three hundred shots per minute.

Having thus fully, clearly, and exactly described the construction and operation of my invention, the following is what I claim as new therein and desire to secure by Letters Patent:

1. Making the series of barrels with their appropriate locks and cartridge-cavities to revolve on an axis, while the requisite motions to perform the loading directly into the rear end of the barrel, exploding, and the cartridge-case-retracting operations are obtained by the impingement of points on the revolving mechanism upon fixed spirals, cams, or inclined planes, these several operations being performed consecutively without stopping the rotation of the barrels when the gun is in operation.

2. The locks, Figs. 12 and 13, which revolve with the barrels and breech, and are operated by the cam-faces and springs during their revolution.

3. The cam-ring, Fig. 5, which is rigidly attached to the diaphragm of the stationary casing, and which by means of its cam-faces controls the longitudinal reciprocating motions of the locks by means of the lugs and the impingement of the butt-ends of the lock upon it, substantially as described.

4. The caps to be placed over the cavity in the carrier to shut off the feed, substantially as described.

RICHARD J. GATLING.

Witnesses:
JOHN CONDELL,
EDWARD H. DWIGHT.

R. J. Gatling
Machine Gun.
Sheet 1. 2 Sheets.
Nº 47631.
Patented May 9. 1865
Fig. 1.

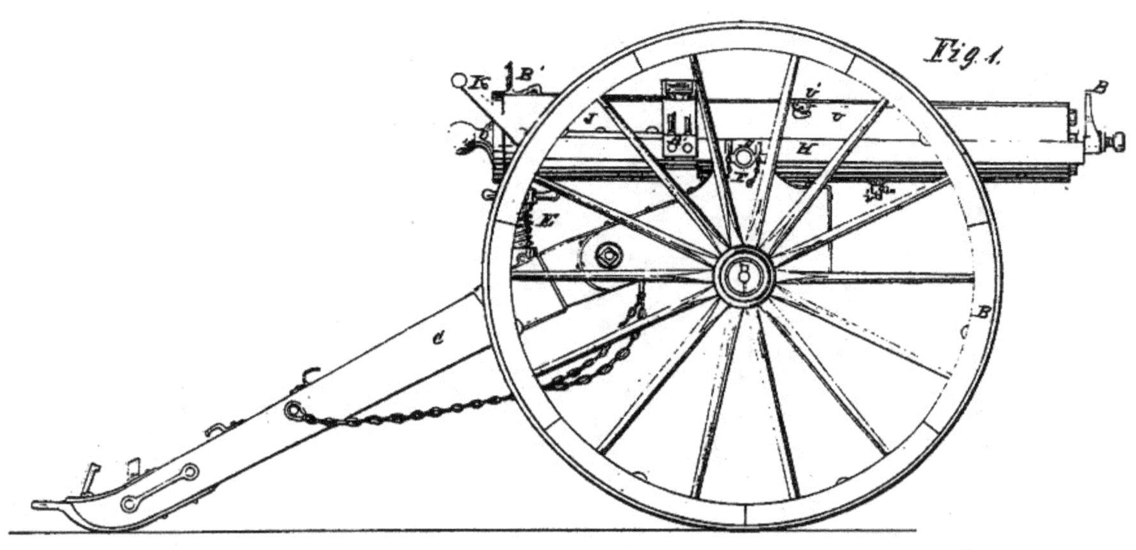

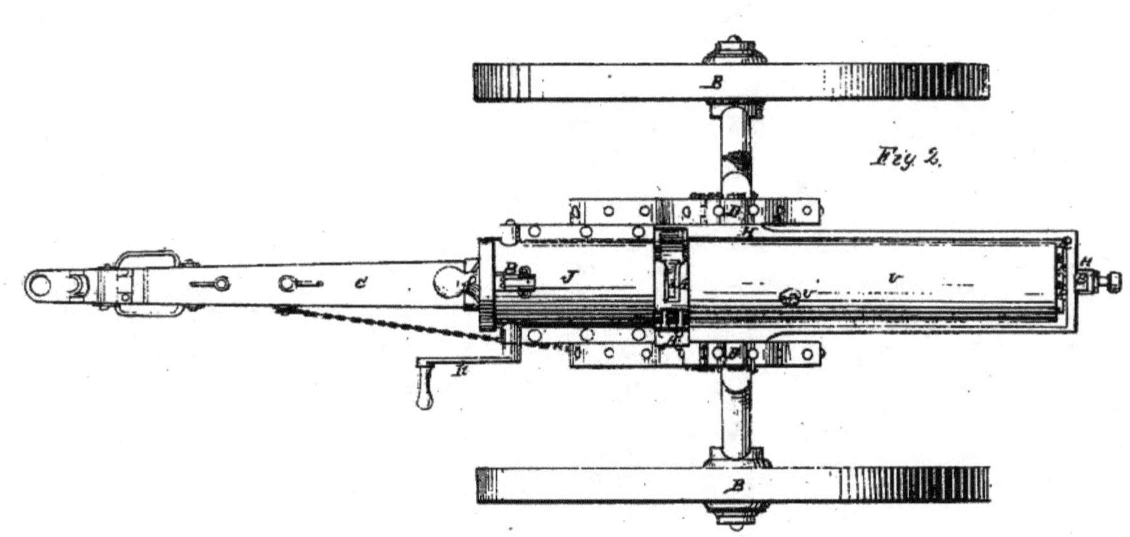

Fig. 2.
Inventor
Richard J. Gatling.

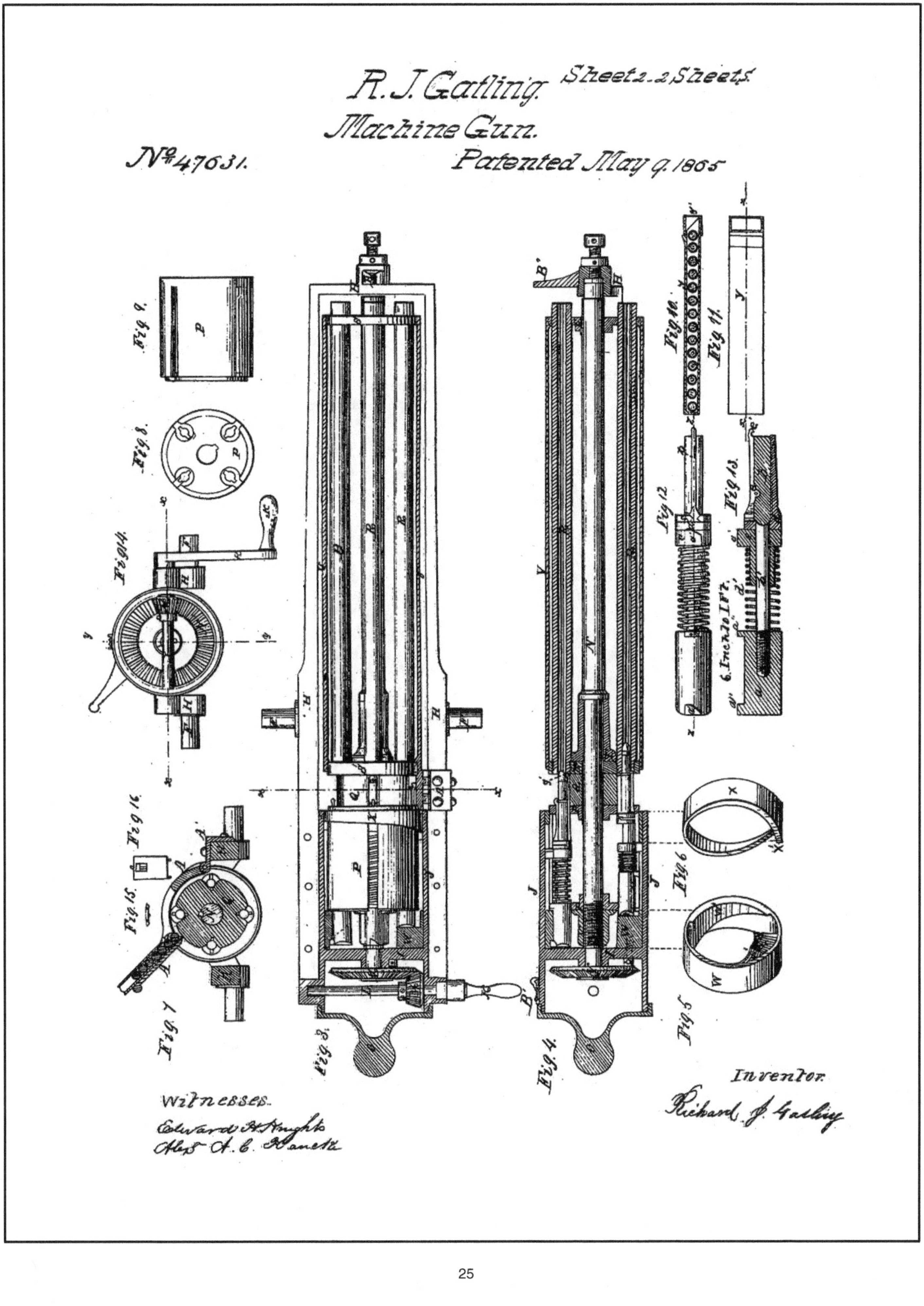
R. J. Gatling. Sheet 2-2 Sheets.
Machine Gun.
No 47631.
Patented May 9. 1865
Fig. 9.
Fig. 8.
Fig. 14.
Fig. 16.
Fig. 15.
Fig. 7
Fig. 3.
Fig. 4.
Fig. 10.
Fig. 11.
Fig. 12
Fig. 13.
6. Inches 1 Ft.
Fig. 6
Fig. 5
Witnesses.
Edward H. Knight
Alex A. C. Klauck
Inventor.
Richard J. Gatling

United States Patent Office.

RICHARD JORDAN GATLING, OF INDIANAPOLIS, INDIANA.

Letters Patent No. 112,138, dated February 28, 1871.

IMPROVEMENT IN REVOLVING-BATTERY GUNS.

The Schedule referred to in these Letters Patent and making part of the same.

To all whom it may concern:

Be it known that I, RICHARD JORDAN GATLING, of Indianapolis, in the county of Marion and State of Indiana, have invented a new and improved Revolving-Battery Gun; and I do hereby declare that the following is a full, clear, and exact description thereof, which will enable others skilled in the art to make and use the same, reference being had to the accompanying drawing forming part of this specification.

This invention relates to certain improvements in the continuous acting revolving-battery gun for which Letters Patent for the United States, numbered 47,631, were granted to me on the 9th day of May, 1865.

The object of this present invention is to perfect the mechanism described in the aforesaid Letters Patent in such manner that more satisfactory operation, greater strength and durability, and simpler construction, will be obtained.

The invention consists, chiefly, in making the "cocking-cam" laterally adjustable, so that the same may, while experiments are made with the gun, without firing the same, be drawn out, to not snap the locks, and that it may also be easily set in to operate the locks when firing is to be carried on. The cocking-cam is also made longitudinally adjustable for the purpose of varying thereby the force of the spring which operates the lock-hammer. Some kinds of cartridges are made of thicker metal than others, and require, consequently, stronger blows, in order to explode their fulminates. It is, therefore, very essential that the blow should be regulated in accordance with the material of which the cartridges are made.

The invention consists, also, in perforating the cascabel-plate and the back diaphragm in the outer casing, and in closing the apertures through both these plates by a removable plug, for the purpose of enabling the removal and reinsertion of either one or more of the locks without requiring the cascabel-plate to be taken off. The repair or inspection of all parts of the gun is thereby considerably facilitated.

The invention consists, further, in enlarging the diameters of the movable locks at their front ends, so that the said locks will be of equal diameter throughout their entire lengths, whereby greater strength and durability are obtained, and in correspondingly increasing the apertures in the front end of the lock-cylinder for the passage of such enlarged locks.

Finally, the invention consists in the use of convenient devices for automatically opening the feed-box which contains the cartridges as soon as the same is inserted in the hopper.

In the accompanying drawing—

Figure 1 represents a plan or top view of my battery-gun.

Figure 2 is a side view of the same.

Figure 3 is a front elevation, partly in section, of the same.

Figure 4 is a rear elevation, partly in section, of the same, without the cascabel-plate.

Figure 5 is a detail side view, on an enlarged scale, of one of the locks.

Figure 6 is a detail front end view of the same.

Figure 7 is a longitudinal section of the same, the plane of section being indicated by the line $x\,x$, fig. 5.

Figure 8 is a transverse section of the same, taken on the plane of the line $y\,y$, fig. 7.

Figure 9 is a detail side view of the double-lever extractor-hook.

Figure 10 is a detail side view of the cartridge feed-box.

Figure 11 is a horizontal longitudinal section of the gun.

Figure 12 is a detail longitudinal section of the breech-case.

Figure 13 is a plan view of the cocking mechanism.

Figure 14 is a transverse section of the same.

Figure 15 is a side view of the cascabel-plug.

Figure 16 is a top view of the same section of the same.

Figure 17 is a front view of the carrier-block, lock-cylinder, hopper, and feed-box, the latter being in section.

Figure 18 is a detail transverse section of the feed-box and hopper.

Similar letters of reference indicate corresponding parts.

A in the drawing represents the axial or main shaft of the gun.

It is journaled at its front end in a transverse bar, m, of the supporting-frame B, and near its rear end in the partition or diaphragm b of the stationary cylindrical breech-case C.

The breech-case C has at its sides longitudinal projecting ribs $c\,c$, which rest upon and are supported by the side bars of the frame B, and which serve to hold the said case stationary.

The frame B has, at or near the middle of the gun, downwardly-projecting arms $d\,d$, which hold under the gun a horizontal plate or turn-table, e, as is clearly shown in figs. 2 and 3.

The plate e is, by a vertical pin or bolt, f, pivoted to a plate, g, which has at its sides the projecting trunnions h.

The trunnions are hung into a suitable gun-carriage. Around the pin f the gun can be swung horizontally, and on the trunnions vertically.

The vertical adjustment is produced by a screw under the breech end of the gun, as usual, while a horizontal screw, i, hung in arms j, that project backward from the plate g, and fitted though a nut, k, serves to adjust the gun horizontally around the pin f.

The trunnions may, if desired, be formed on the frame B, in which case the horizontal adjustment can only be produced by setting the entire gun-carriage.

l is the front sight, secured upon the front cross-bar m of the frame B, and

n is the rear sight, secured upon the case C or upon the cascabel-plate D, which is screwed to the same.

The shaft A has two flanges, o p, one in front, somewhat behind the bar m, and the other near the middle.

In these flanges are secured the barrels E E.

The barrels are with their rear ends screwed into the rear flange p, as in fig. 11, where their front ends are fitted loose through apertures in the front flange o, to be merely supported by the same.

The flanges o p are firmly secured to the shaft A, so that they will revolve with the same and carry the barrels around with it.

There are six barrels shown in the drawing. Any other suitable number may, however, be employed.

Directly in rear of the flange p is mounted, upon the shaft A, the carrier-block F, which is to receive the cartridges from the feed-box.

This block has as many longitudinal grooves g g as there are barrels E, one groove in line with each barrel. The grooves are of suitable form, preferably as in fig. 17, and should be adapted to the form of cartridges employed.

The grooves are so set that a cartridge placed into one of them can, by longitudinal motion of a rammer or rod from behind, be conveniently pushed into the barrel pertaining thereto, the locks forming such rammers, as hereinafter more fully described.

Directly in rear of the carrier-block F is mounted, upon the shaft A, the lock-cylinder G, which, with its front end, is about in line with the case C, while its length is about half that of the said case.

The cylinder G has as many longitudinal perforations as there are barrels, and the axes of such perforations are in line with the grooves g in F, and of the barrels.

The perforations in the cylinder are entirely cylindrical, that is to say, of equal diameters from end to end, to receive the locks H H, which are also of cylindrical form, as indicated in fig. 7.

Directly in rear of the lock-cylinder G is screwed, upon the shaft A, a nut, I, which serves to firmly secure the flange p, carrier F, and cylinder G together, and which, when withdrawn, permits their removal from the shaft.

Between the nut I and the diaphragm b of the case C is arranged the stationary cam J, by which the locks are longitudinally adjusted in the cylinder G. This cam is firmly secured in the case C, so that it will remain stationary with the same, while the shaft A with the nut I and its other appendages is free to revolve. The cam is of annular form, and surrounds the nut I, as shown in fig. 11, by which arrangement considerable room is economized.

Between the diaphragm b and the cascabel-plate D is mounted, upon the extreme rear end of the shaft A, a worm-wheel, L, whose diameter is not larger than that of the carrier-block F, so that an aperture may be made through the diaphragm for reaching the locks.

A worm, r, formed on a transverse shaft, s, that is hung in the rear part of the case A, engages in the teeth of the wheel L, as in fig. 4.

By means of a crank, t, on said shaft s, the same can be readily revolved, and will thereby also revolve the shaft A and all the appendages of the same, to wit, the nut I, cylinder G, block F, flanges o p, and barrels E, the latter revolving around and with the shaft A, but not around their own axes.

The locks H are of the following construction:

Each lock is made in form of a cylindrical shell, slightly longer than the combined length of the cylinder G and block F. The front part of each lock is nearly solid, having only a small longitudinal central bore for the reception of the firing-pin u. The rear part of the lock, however, forms a cylindrical chamber for the reception of the hammer-spring v, as is clearly shown in fig. 7.

The firing-pin u is, with its rear end, dovetailed and firmly secured into a rod, w, which is called the lock-hammer.

The spring v bears with its rear end against a shoulder, x, of the lock-case H, and with its front end against a shoulder or sleeve, y, of the lock-hammer, it having, therefore, the tendency to push the lock-hammer forward, so that the front end of the firing-pin will project from the front end of the lock H, as in figs. 5 and 7.

When the lock-hammer is thus pushed forward its shoulder y rests against a front inner shoulder, z, of the shell H, as shown.

From the shoulder y projects through the side of the shell H, and also through the cylinder G, a lug, a', which is acted upon by the cocking apparatus, as hereinafter more fully described.

In order to permit the longitudinal motion of the lock-hammer and firing-pin, and consequently, also, that of the lug a', the lock H and cylinder G must both be longitudinally slotted to let the lug pass backward and forward. Each lock H is therefore longitudinally slotted, and the cylinder has as many slots of equal length as there are locks and barrels.

On the rear end of each lock H is a projecting ear, b', which fits into the double inclined or spiral groove or channel of the stationary cam J, and which, as the cylinder G is revolved with the locks, slides in said inclined or spiral groove, and causes the required reciprocating motion of the locks by which the cartridges are forced into the barrels, the breech ends of the latter closed, and the empty cartridge-shells withdrawn.

In order to prevent the locks from turning in the cylinder G, they have each ribs or ears c', fitting into and sliding in longitudinal grooves of the nut I, and other ribs d', fitting into longitudinal grooves formed at the bottoms of the main grooves of the carrier-block F.

In figs. 5 and 17, these latter ribs d' are clearly shown.

When the lock is pushed forward to close the breech-end of the barrel, the bar M strikes the collar of the cartridge and is first moved back, and then, owing to the inclined front edge of the hook h', swung up and covers the said collar, so that the latter is engaged by the hook.

When the lock is moved back again by the cam J, the hook draws the cartridge-shell back with it, but the bar M is first drawn forward on the lock to fit the inclined edge of the ear g' against that of its recess, as in fig. 17. Thereby the bar M is locked down so that it cannot spring up to again release the cartridge-shell. The latter is thereby safely withdrawn from the barrel.

The slot of the ear e' is therefore of great importance, as by its means the retractor-bar can be locked down to retain the cartridge-shell, and again liberated to let the hook swing over the head of the cartridge.

The extractor shown in fig. 9 consists of a lever, M', and spring-holder a''. The latter is secured in a groove of the lock, and fits with its inclined front end under the rear arm of the lever M'.

The lever is, by a pin, b'', pivoted to the lock, the said pivot passing through a longitudinal slot in an ear, c'' of the lever. The slot allows slight longitudinal play to the lever M' when the same strikes the cartridge-head, and when it commences to withdraw the shell.

The spring holds its hook h' over the flange of the

shell, and prevents it from slipping off, permitting it, however, to swing while it engages said shoulder.

The cocking apparatus is more clearly illustrated in figs. 12, 13, and 14. It is mainly an inclined or spiral plate, N, arranged on the inner side of the breech-case C, so that the lug a', when the lock is moved forward, may be arrested by the same, and the spring v gradually contracted and the firing-pin drawn back into the lock-shell H.

When the lug a' passes the end of the stationary plate N, it is suddenly released, and the spring v with it, causing the latter to expand and to suddenly and violently force the firing-pin forward against the cartridge to explode the same.

The plate N is stationary on the case C, while the lugs a' revolve with the cylinder G. The plate N will, therefore, act upon the firing-pins in the several locks successively, and will cause the successive discharge of the barrels as the same arrive in line with it.

The plate N may be arranged on any suitable part of the cylinder G, either above, below, or on either side of the shaft A. In the drawing it is represented as being on the side of the cylinder.

In order to permit the lateral adjustment of the cocking-plate N, the same is secured to a slide, i', which projects into one of the ribs c, and which has an aperture to receive the eccentric j', on a vertical arbor, l'.

The said arbor is fitted vertically into the rib c, as shown. By turning it, the eccentric will draw the slide i' in or out, as may be desired, drawing thereby also the plate N into or out of gear with the several lugs a'.

The arbor can be so operated by hand that the plate N can be moved into or out of gear, as may be desired. Thus exercise of the gun by recruits, &c., is permitted without snapping the locks.

By connecting the slide with a longitudinal screw, d'', which is fitted through ears on the rib c, as in fig. 13, the plate N may be made longitudinally adjustable for the purpose of compressing the springs v to a greater or lesser degree, and of consequently regulating the force with which the firing-pin is projected against the cartridge.

A sliding bolt may be arranged on the case for locking the shaft l', and with it the cocking-plate N, in either one of the desired positions.

In order to allow the removal and insertion of each lock without requiring the removal of the cascabel-plate, there is an aperture, n, through the cascabel-plate, and in line with the same a similar aperture, o', through the diaphragm b.

Both these apertures can be closed by a plug, P, which is inserted from behind into the plate D, as is clearly shown in fig. 11.

The gear-wheel L is made small enough to permit the arrangement of the said apertures n' o', and plug P, in line with the locks.

The plug carries at its front end a sleeve, p, which has a projecting grooved arm, a, that is fitted into a recess of the cam J, the groove in a forming a continuation or completion of the groove in said cam, in which the ears b' of the locks move.

A nose, r', on the plug P, locks behind the cascabel-plate and holds the plug in place. When the latter is turned to bring the nose r' into line with a notch, s', that enlarges the aperture n' of the cascabel-plate, (fig. 11,) the plug can be withdrawn. Thereby the apertures n' o' are opened, and each lock as it arrives in line with the same can be withdrawn and reinserted. The repair and inspection of the locks are thereby facilitated, and the gun can be kept in perfect repair while in service, without requiring the removal of the heavier parts.

In order to facilitate the removal of the plug, P

that is to say, the turning of the same, a lever may be attached to the end of the plug, to form a crank on the same.

Upon the frame B is secured a curved plate, R, which covers partly the carrier-block F, and which, at its outer upper end has a hopper, S, formed on it, for the reception of the feed-box T, which is the box containing the cartridges to be fired.

The box T is a curved or straight sheet-metal case of suitable height, its width and length corresponding with that of the cartridges to be used.

At one end this case has a hinged bottom, t', which is held closed by a hook on a pivoted lever, V, that is acted upon by a spring, u', as in figs. 17 and 18.

When the case T is inserted into the hopper, the inner face of the hook v' of the lever V is moved on an inclined face, w' of the hopper, so that the hook is drawn off the bottom t', causing the same to drop open, as in fig. 17, and to liberate the cartridges W, which will be taken up by the carrier-block F as the grooves of the same are brought successively under the case T.

A lug, x', on the case T, strikes against a nose, y', of the hopper, when the case has been inserted sufficiently far.

When a feed-box has been emptied, it is withdrawn from the hopper and another one put into its place, the empty one being readily refilled to be ready for further use.

I prefer to have the case T curved, as in fig. 10, and a weight, U, in it, to rest on the cartridges, so that the weight will have less effect when the case is full than when the same is nearly empty.

A full box, T, is placed into the hopper S, so that its cartridges will be liberated. The plug P is put and locked into the cascabel-plate and diaphragm, so that its flange s'' abuts against the face of the cascabel-plate.

The cocking-plate N is put into gear to act on the lugs a', and the shaft s is revolved. The cartridges are thereby successively fed into the grooves of the carrier-block F.

As soon as a groove, q, has been filled, the lock H in line with it is gradually moved forward by the cam J, and the cartridge pushed into the barrel E, pertaining to and in line with such lock.

When a cartridge has been fully inserted, the breech-end of the barrel is closed by the lock H, and then the firing-pin is violently thrown forward by the spring v, to explode the fulminate in the cartridge, and by the same ignite the charge.

While the lock was being pushed forward, the lug a' was detained by and moved along on the cocking-plate N, whereby the spring v was compressed and the firing-pin drawn into the shell H.

At the same that the lock H closed the breech of the barrel the lug a' passed the plate N' and liberated the firing-pin, which was propelled as stated.

While the lock passed forward to close the breech of the barrel, the hook of the retractor M was slipped over the head of the cartridge, and remained in that position during the operation of firing.

After firing the lock is gradually drawn back by the cam J, and the hook of M draws the empty cartridge-shell back with it.

Another lock, barrel, and cartridge arrive in line with the cocking-plate N, and are acted upon as aforesaid.

When a lock is out of order and firing can be ceased, the plug P is taken out and the shaft A turned until such damaged lock arrives in line with the apertures n' o', when the same can be withdrawn and repaired, and a new lock put into its place.

Whenever, during the revolution of the shaft A, a lock, H, is quite drawn back, a cartridge drops into the groove g in front of it.

4

Having thus described my invention,

I claim as new and desire to secure by Letters Patent—

1. The cocking-plate or cam N, arranged laterally adjustable in the breech-case of the gun, substantially as and for the purpose set forth.

2. The arbor l', eccentric j, and slide i', in combination with the laterally-adjustable cocking-plate N, all arranged as set forth.

3. The cocking-plate N, arranged longitudinally, adjustable to permit the regulation of the firing-spring v, as set forth.

4. The perforated cascabel-plate D, in combination with the perforated diaphragm-plate b, relatively constructed and arranged, as and for the purpose set forth.

5. The plug P, in combination with the perforated cascabel-plate D, and perforated diaphragm-plate b, all relatively constructed and arranged as and for the purpose heretofore specified.

6. The worm-gear or its equivalent, of less diameter than the circle described by the locks, in combination with the perforations in the diaphragm and cascabel-plate, to permit the removal of the locks, in the manner and for the purpose described.

7. The plug P, having the lug and ring with lip projection, the latter having an inner transverse groove in which the rear lugs of the locks work when the gun is revolved, the said plug not being designed to receive any part of the force of the charge, but used with its appendages for the purpose of preventing the locks from working forward or backward at the time they are passing the slot in the rear cam, and the perforation in the diaphragm during the revolution of the gear, all as described.

8. The cylindrically-formed locks H, working in uniform-sized perforations, made longitudinally and entirely through a revolving lock-cylinder, in contradistinction to locks and perforations reduced in diameter at their front parts, as shown and described in my patent dated August 9, 1865.

9. The lever V, acted upon by the spring u' to hold the bottom t' closed, and allow it to be automatically opened when its lower part comes in contact with the hopper, in combination with the feed-box T, for the use and purpose specified.

10. The nut I, arranged on the shaft A, to hold the carrier-block F and cylinder G in place, and to act as guide for the locks, substantially as specified.

RICHARD J. GATLING.

Witnesses:
H. CLAY,
THOMAS L. SULLIVAN.

R. J. GATLING.
REVOLVING BATTERY GUN.

No. 112,138.   Patented Feb. 28, 1871.

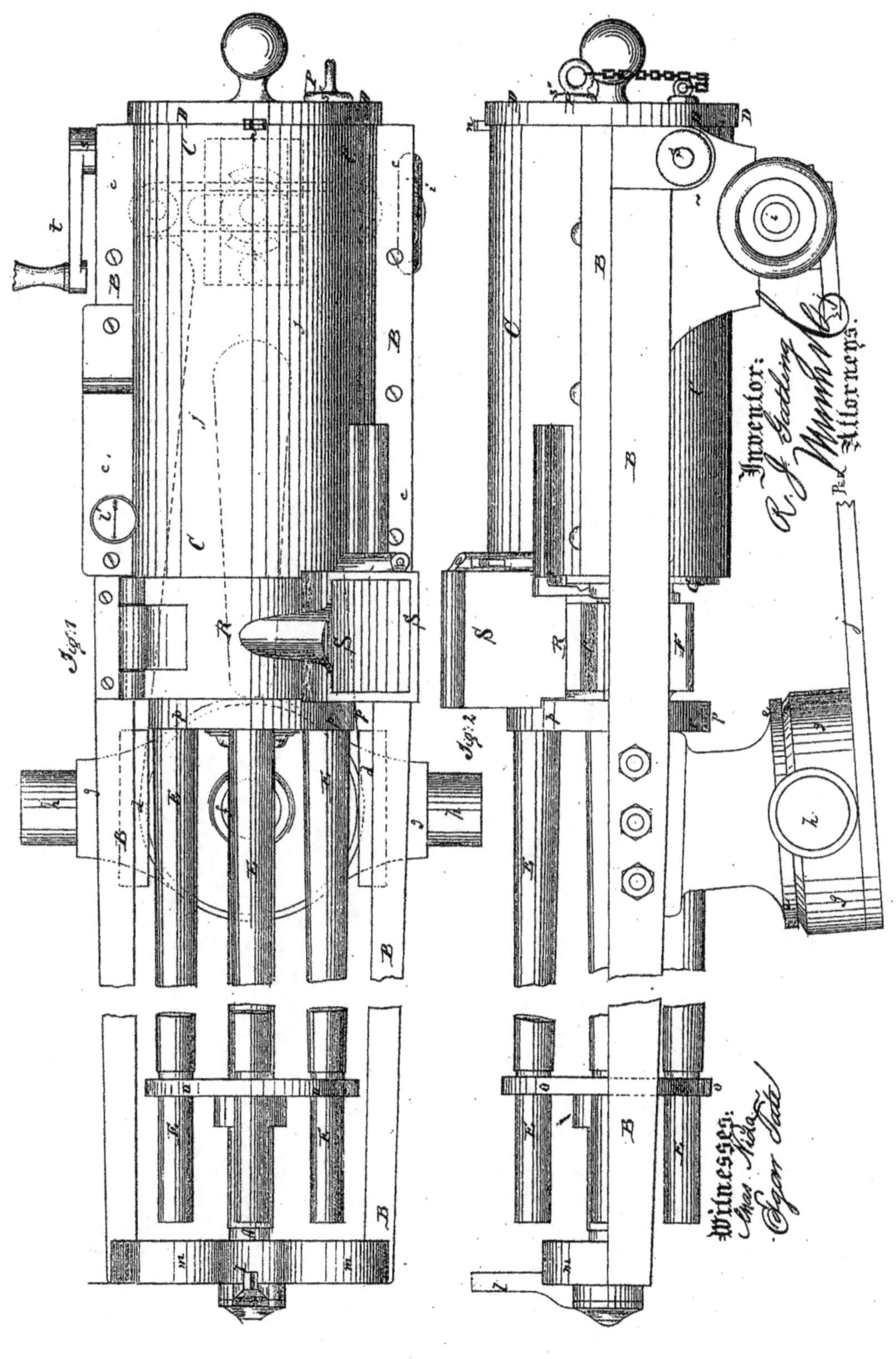

R. J. GATLING.
REVOLVING BATTERY GUN.

No. 112,138.　　　　　　　　　Patented Feb. 28, 1871.

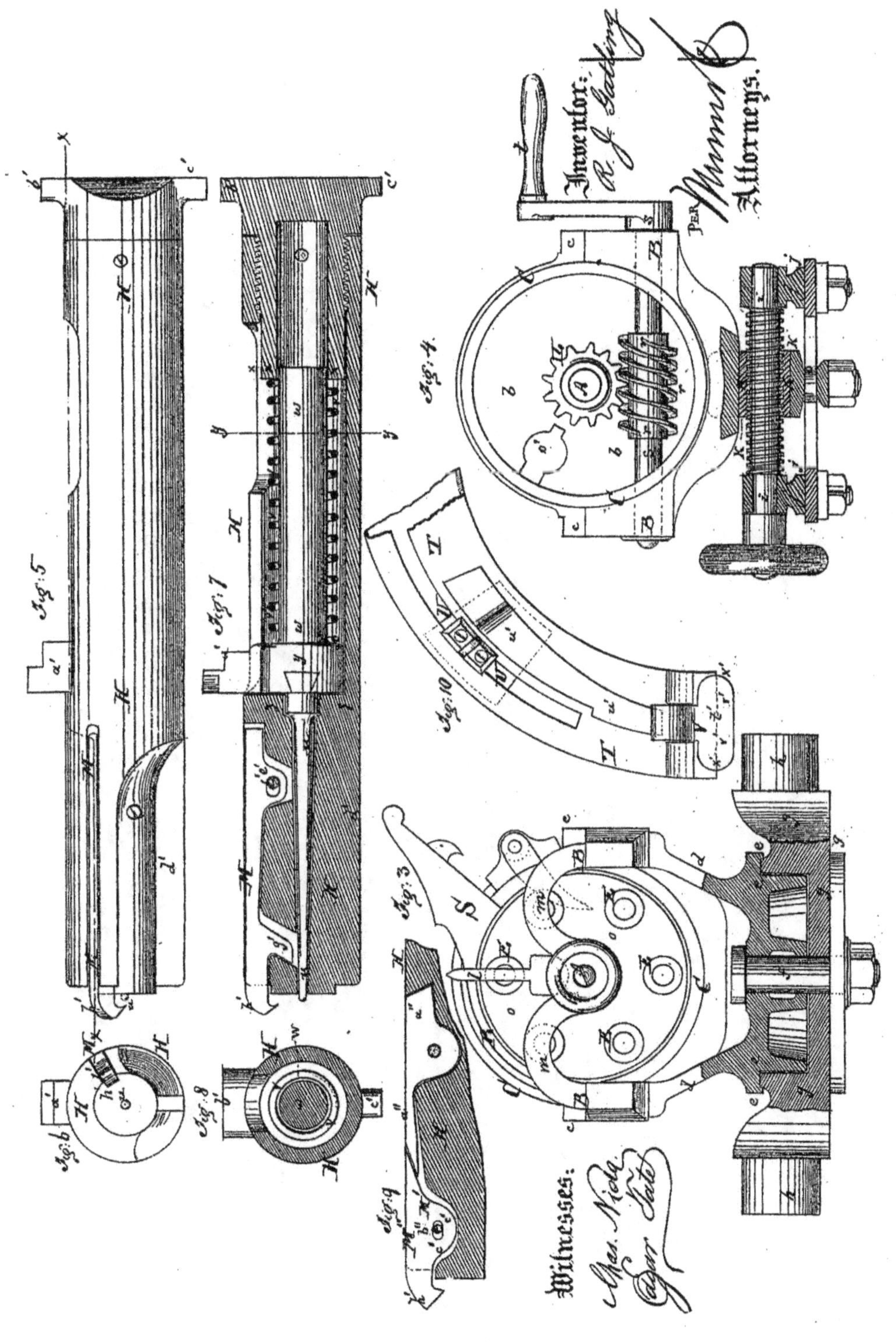

R. J. GATLING.
REVOLVING BATTERY GUN.

No. 112,138.   Patented Feb. 28, 1871.

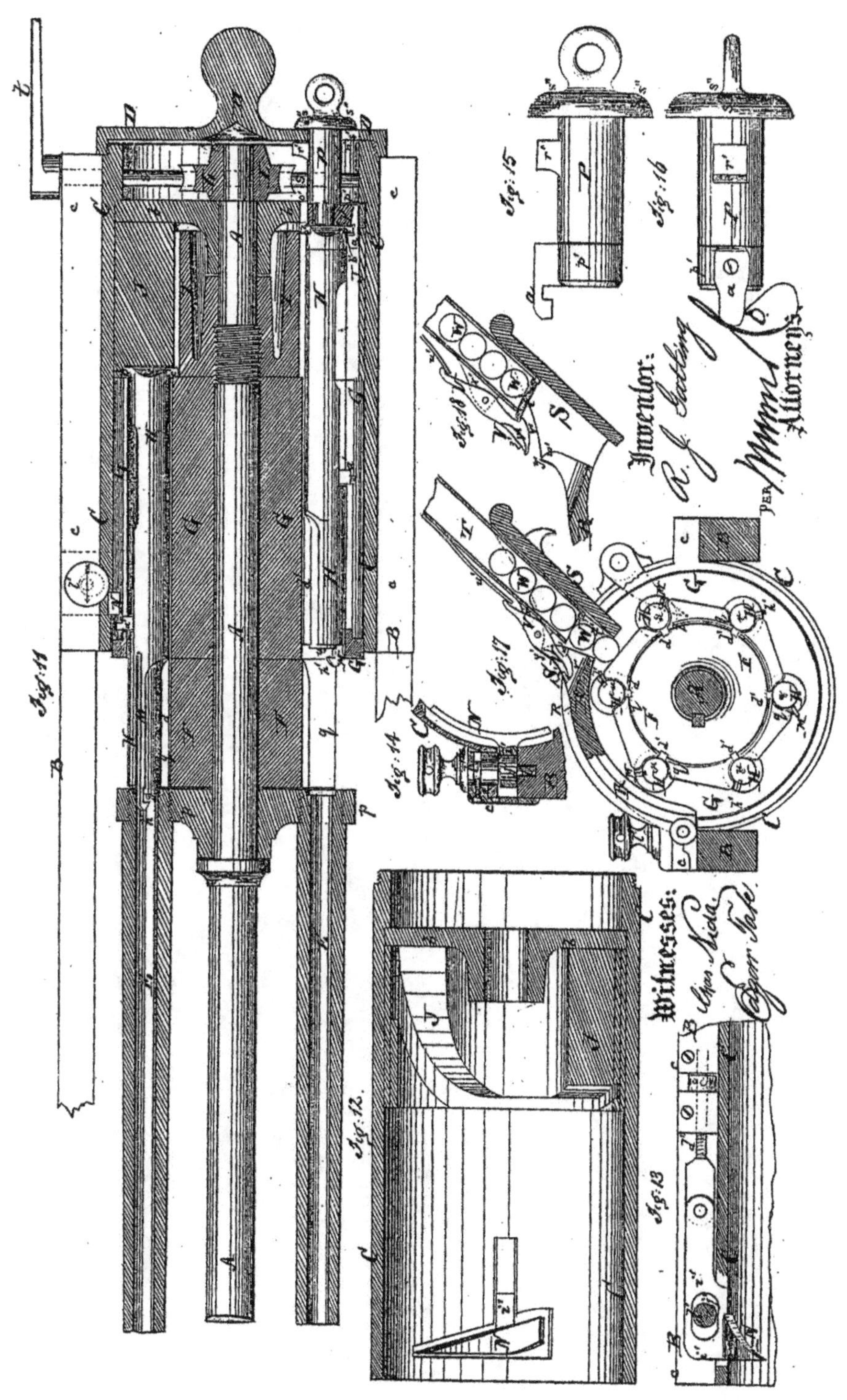

UNITED STATES PATENT OFFICE.

RICHARD J. GATLING, OF HARTFORD, CONNECTICUT.

IMPROVEMENT IN REVOLVING-BATTERY GUNS.

Specification forming part of Letters Patent No. 125,563, dated April 9, 1872.

Specification describing an Improved Revolving-Battery Gun, invented by RICHARD JORDAN GATLING, of Hartford, in the county of Hartford and State of Connecticut.

This invention relates to several improvements on the "Gatling Revolving - Battery Gun," for which two Letters Patent of the United States, numbered 47,631 and 112,138, were respectively granted on the 9th day of May, 1865, and 28th day of February, 1871. The object of the present invention is principally to reduce the length of lock and consequent length of breech-case, and thereby diminish the weight, expense, and difficulty of manufacture of the entire gun. In this case I employ a detaining device provided with a transverse groove to receive the knobs on the rear end of the lock-hammers or firing-pins, and prevent them moving forward with the locks themselves, so that when said knobs, in consequence of the continued circular movement of the locks, escape from said groove, the spiral spring encircling the firing-pins shall cause them to deliver a sudden and powerful blow against the butt of the cartridge, and thus occasion the desired explosion and consequent discharge. The construction of the lock itself is modified in conformity with the aforementioned mechanism by providing the lock-hammer with an interior shoulder for the spring to bear against, and with a knob at the outer end for the grip of the detaining-cam. My invention also consists in an improved construction of the breech-case, lock-cylinder, and also of the carrier-block, with the view of adapting the same for the reception of the improved locks, the carrier-block being made hollow to reduce weight and cost of material.

In the accompanying drawing, Figure 1 represents a longitudinal section of the breech part of the gun, showing the improved arrangement of parts. Fig. 2 is a longitudinal section of the lock. Figs. 3 and 4 are transverse sections of the same on the lines $c\,c$ and $c\,k$, Fig. 2, respectively. Fig. 5 is a detail side view of the lock-hammer. Fig. 6 is a transverse section, and Fig. 7 an end view of the head, which is screwed upon the lock-hammer. Fig. 8 is a front-end view of the breech-case, with the lock - cylinder and appendages removed. Figs. 9 and 10 are longitudinal sections of the same on the line $k\,c$, Fig. 8, look-

ing in the direction of the arrows 1 and 2, respectively. Fig. 11 is a detail transverse section on the line $k\,k$, Fig. 8, showing how the lock-hammer or firing-pin is held back in the detaining-cam. Fig. 12 is a vertical transverse section of the lock-cylinder and breech-case, the line $c\,q$ in Figs. 1 and 9 indicating the plane of section. Fig. 13 is a vertical transverse section of the carrier-block, the line $q\,q$ in Fig. 1 indicating the plane of section.

Similar letters of reference indicate corresponding parts.

A in the drawing represents the cylindrical breech-case, secured upon the frame of the gun, which is mounted in suitable manner either upon a gun-carriage, tripod, or other suitable support. In this breech-case is the diaphragm a and cascabel-plate b, between which a chamber for the reception of the worm and worm-wheel is formed. B is the axial shaft of the gun. It is hung substantially as described in my former patents, and serves to hold the barrels C C, the carrier-block D, and the lock-cylinder E, which revolve with it whenever it is turned by means of the crank-handle d, which imparts motion to the worm. F F are the locks, and G is the hopper-plate or cover of the carrier-block, with an aperture through which the cartridges are supplied to the latter. Within the breech-case are arranged the stationary spiral or inclined cams e and f, for forcing the locks forward and back. These cam-grooves or tracks are formed on a cylindrical shell, H, which is fitted within the breech-case and secured thereto by a longitudinal screw, v, that passes through the diaphragm a. By means of this screw the shell, with its cams, is held securely to its place. e is the cam-groove or track, whereon the locks are forced forward. Its front end is, by a non-spiral portion, g, joined to the front end of the retracting-cam f. Directly behind the junction of e and g is arranged the detaining-cam I. The same is a curved plate having a dovetail shank, h, which enters a corresponding groove in an inwardly-projecting ear or block, i, of the shell H. A spring, j, placed between the diaphragm a and shank h, serves to force the detaining cam forward, so that the upper end of its curved face will come against the cam e, but permits the same to move backward for purposes hereinafter specified. The face of the detaining-cam I has a countersunk groove, of such cross-section as most conveniently to receive the knob at the end of the lock - hammer, and as indicated in Fig. 11. Each lock F consists of a shell, *l*, and lock-hammer *m*, as principal parts. The lock-hammer or firing-pin has the firing-pin formed at its front end, as is clearly shown in Fig. 5, and a knob, *n*, at its rear end, said knob being intended to fit the countersunk grooves of the detaining-cam. A spiral spring is placed within the shell *l* and around the lock-hammer or firing-pin, between a shoulder or head, *o*, on the latter, and a screw-plug, *p*, at the back end of the shell. The head *o* is screwed upon the lock-hammer or firing-pin, and is by the spiral spring held against the front end of the chamber in the shell. If the knob *n* is taken hold of and drawn back the spring will be contracted to violently propel the firing-pin-forward whenever the knob is released. *r* is the cartridge-shell extractor, applied to the lock, and *s* the projecting lug on the lock, that moves along the cams *e f*, and thereby causes the forward and backward motion of the lock. *t* is a dovetail tenon on the lock-shell, fitting into corresponding grooves of the lock-cylinder and carrier-block, as indicated in Figs. 12 and 13. The carrier-block as well as the lock-cylinder, it will be seen, are cast or formed hollow, with supporting disks or arms that hold them to the shaft. Considerable weight and material are thereby economized. From the front end of the lock-cylinder projects a flange, *u*, perforated to admit the locks, and made circular at the outer edge to fit and support the breech-case. The locks, when held by the grooved lock-cylinder, are with their projecting lugs *s s* in such contact with the cams, tracks, or grooves *e f*, respectively, that they will, when revolved by the rotation of the lock-cylinder, be also moved forward and backward in the requisite manner to push the cartridges into the barrels, explode the charges, and withdraw the shells, substantially as specified in my former Letters Patent. When a lock approaches (along the cam *e*) its foremost position the knob *n* of its lock-hammer or firing-pin enters the upper end of the groove in the detaining-cam I. This cam is held against *e* and beveled at its upper end, that the knob may conveniently enter its groove. As the lock continues to advance, the cam I, however, detaining the knob *n* in the same vertical plane, it is evident that the firing-pin will be automatically drawn back within the lock and the spring contracted. As soon as the lock arrives in line with the inner or lower end of the detaining-cam I the knob is released by the latter and the lock-hammer or firing-pin propelled forward to explode the charge. In this manner the charges of the barrels are successively fired with the utmost precision and regularity. The cam I

may, if desired, be continued more or less far around, at such a distance from the tracks *e f* as to hold the point of the firing-pin slightly drawn in, except when in the act of firing. When the shaft is turned in the wrong direction the knobs will strike the face of the cams I and push it back against the spring *j*, the detaining-cam being prevented thereby from cocking. The plate or face *g* braces the back ends of the locks at the moment of firing, and takes their recoil, being made strong and large for this purpose, as shown.

The arrangement of the automatic detaining-cam in place of the cocking apparatus formerly in use is of great advantage. It permits the dispensing of half the length of lock and breech-case, and consequent reduction of expense and increase of carrying facility. It is not in the way of the proper function of the other mechanism, and is positive in its action.

Having thus described my invention, I claim as new and desire to secure by Letters Patent—

1. A firing-pin detainer, when located or arranged in the breech-case of a revolving gun, between the transverse vertical planes bounding the terminations of lock-guides or tracks, substantially as described, for the purpose of economizing space and operating the locks, as specified.

2. The combination of the detainer I with the cams, tracks, or guides *e* and *g*, as shown and described, whereby the locks are caused to advance while their firing-pins traverse and are held back in the groove of said detainer until liberated to explode the cartridges, as set forth.

3. The lock F, consisting essentially of a shell, *l*, provided with a lug, S, and with a tongue adapted to fit and operate as a guide in a groove of the revolving cylinder, and the firing-pin having a knob or its equivalent on its projecting rear end, substantially as specified.

4. A rotary-battery gun, provided with revolving locks whose firing-pins are held back by means of the rear or knob ends of the same engaging with a detaining device, substantially as described.

5. In a revolving-battery gun the combination of the spring *j* with the detainer, whereby it is adapted to yield backward, as shown and described.

6. The combination of the locks F, provided with lugs *s*, and lock-hammers or spring firing-pins *m n*, with the guides *e*, *f*, and *g*, and grooved detaining device I, all constructed, arranged, and operating as specified.

RICHARD J. GATLING.

Witnesses:
    EUGENE D. FISK,
    FREDERICK EBERLE.

R. J. GATLING.
Improvement in Revolving Battery Guns.

No. 125,563.

Patented April 9, 1872.

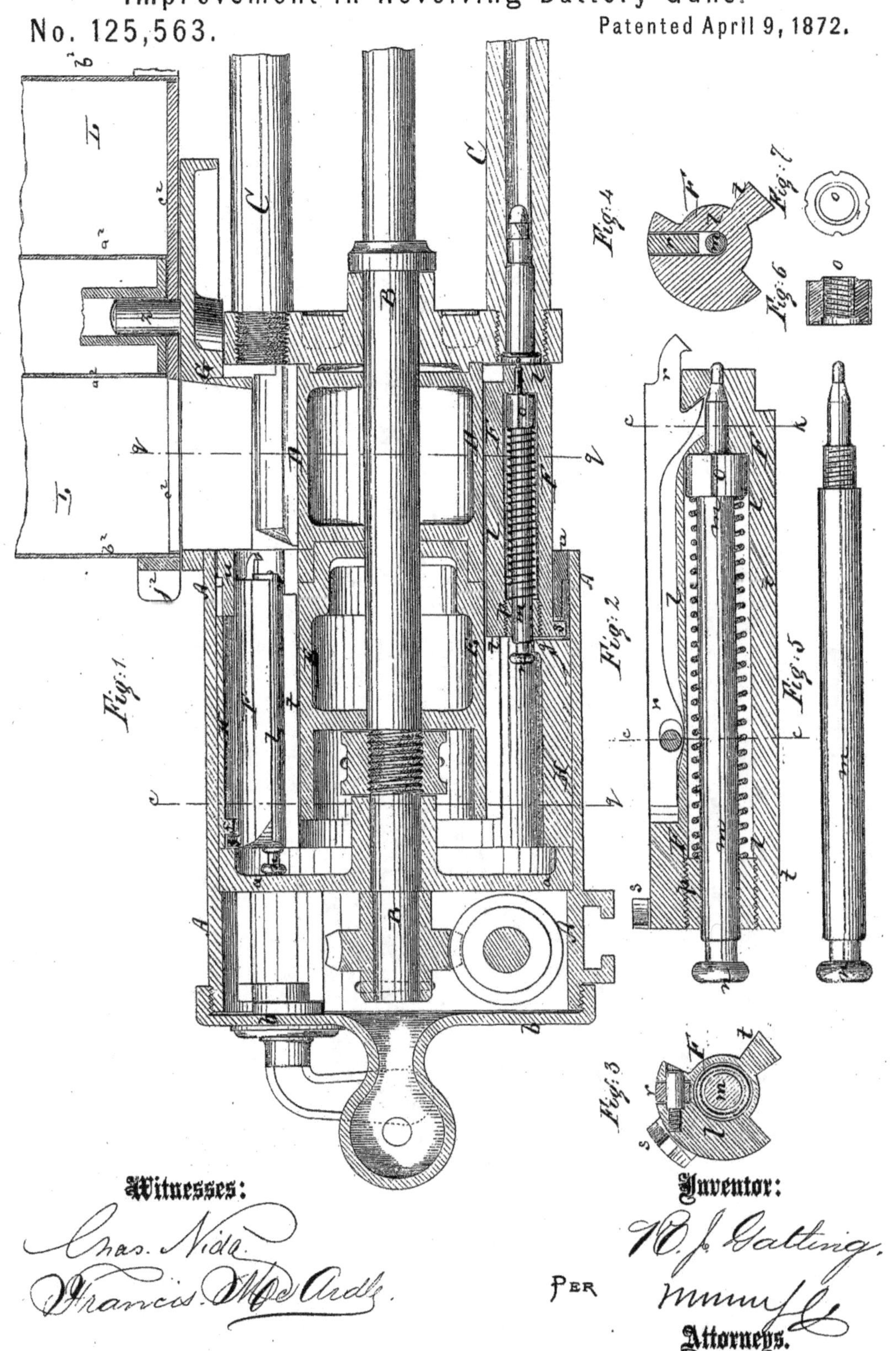

Witnesses:
Chas. Nida.
Francis M. c Ardle.

Inventor:
R. J. Gatling.

Per

Attorneys.

Witnesses:
Chas. Nida
Francis McArdle

Inventor:
R. J. Gatling.
PER
Attorneys.

R. J. GATLING.
Improvement in Revolving Battery Guns.

No. 125,563. Patented April 9, 1872.

Fig. 12.

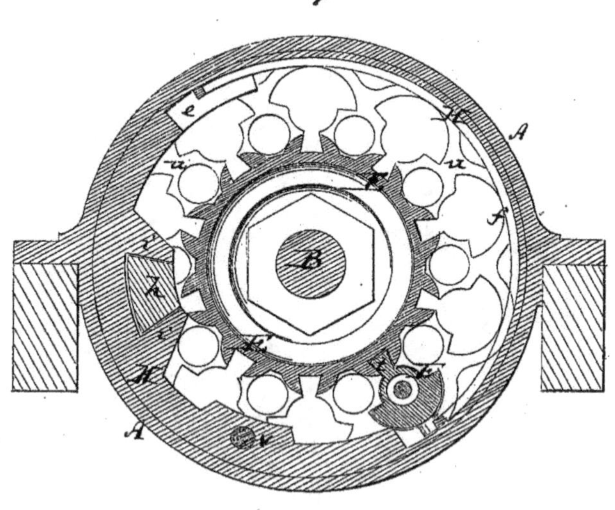

Fig. 13.

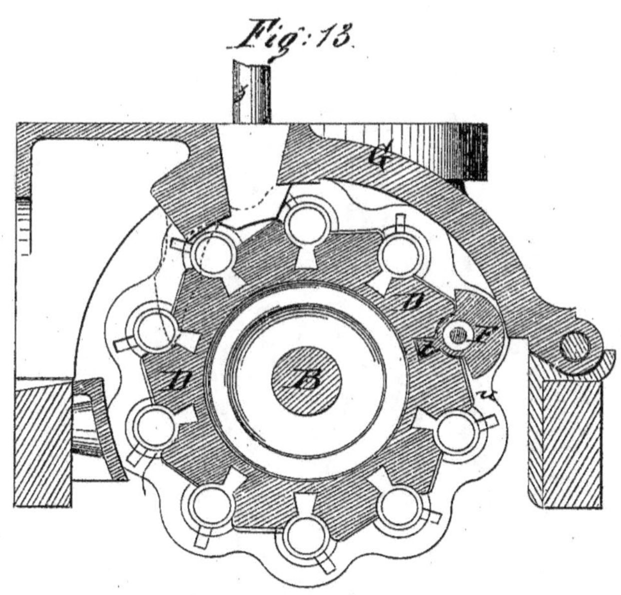

Witnesses:
Chas. Nida
Francis McArdle

Inventor:
R. J. Gatling
PER
Attorneys.

UNITED STATES PATENT OFFICE.

RICHARD J. GATLING, OF HARTFORD, CONNECTICUT.

IMPROVEMENT IN TRAVERSING MECHANISMS FOR MACHINE-GUNS.

Specification forming part of Letters Patent No. **145,563**, dated December 16, 1873; application filed October 25, 1873.

To all whom it may concern:

Be it known that I, RICHARD J. GATLING, of Hartford, in the county of Hartford and State of Connecticut, have invented a new and useful Improvement in Traversing Mechanism for Machine Gun, of which the following is a specification:

Figure 1, Sheet 1, is a rear view of my improved traversing mechanism. Fig. 2, Sheet 1, is a detail top view of a part of the same, part being broken away to show the construction. Fig. 3, Sheet 2, is a cross-section of the same taken through the line $x\,x$, Fig. 2. Fig. 4, Sheet 2, is a longitudinal section of the pin-socket, showing the pin in place. Figs. 5 and 6, Sheet 2, are detail side views of different sizes of the grooved cylinder. Fig. 7, Sheet 2, is a view illustrating the manner in which the shot are thrown.

Similar letters of reference indicate corresponding parts.

The invention will first be fully described, and then pointed out in the claims.

A is a bar or cylinder, upon the upper side of the inner end of which is formed a T-flange, B, to enter a T-groove upon the lower side of the gun, so that the rear end of the gun may slide upon the said flange to give the sweep. In the lower side of the inner end of the cylinder A is formed a transverse groove, C, the cavity of which is a little more than a half-cylinder, to receive the ball formed upon the upper end of the screw, by which the breech of the gun is raised and lowered in sighting it. The cylinder A is perforated longitudinally to receive the screw D, which has a hand-wheel, E, attached to its outer end, and which is swiveled to the said cylinder A. The forward side of the cylinder A is slotted to receive the neck of the nut F, which fits upon the screw D, and is cast upon the rear side of the vertical socket G, in which is fitted a pin, H, which is supported by a lever-catch, I, the toe, formed upon the lower end of which passes in through a hole in the lower part of the socket G, and enters a ring-groove in the lower part of the pin H, to support said pin in place, two grooves being formed in said pin, so that it may be supported in gear and out of gear. The upper end of the lever-catch I is held out by a small spring interposed between it and the socket

G, as shown in Fig. 4. The upper end of the pin H has a friction-sleeve, J, placed upon it to diminish friction, and enters a groove in the cylinder K, which is attached to the forward end of the crank-screw, by which the gun is moved upon its pivot, to discharge it and give it the sweep. In the cylinder K are formed two grooves, $k^1\,k^2$, to receive the end of the pin H. The groove k^1 is straight, as shown in Figs. 1, 5, and 6, and is designed for use when direct firing is required.

When it is desired to sweep a portion of the field with the shot, the end of the pin H is inserted in the cam-groove k^2, which has a cam incline formed in it upon each side of the cylinder K, so that, as the said cylinder is revolved, the gun may be oscillated horizontally to give it the required sweep.

The sweep of the gun may be varied by varying the length of the cylinder K, and consequently of the cams or inclines of the groove k^2. The cylinder shown in Fig. 6 is designed to sweep through the space of one degree, the one shown in Fig. 1 through one and a half degrees, and the one in Fig. 5 through two degrees.

By this construction, if the gun is being fired at a body of troops within the range represented by the full lines in Fig. 7, by turning the screw D a little, the sweep of the gun may be changed so as to be represented by the dotted lines with arrow-heads, and by turning the screw still more, the sweep will be represented by the dotted lines without arrow-heads. In the same way the sweep of the gun may be shifted to the left by turning the screw D in the other direction, so that the sweep of the gun may be changed to follow a moving body of troops without moving the trail, which always necessitates a resighting of the gun.

In the same way, when the gun is used for direct firing, the line of fire may be changed to the right or left by turning the screw D in one or the other direction.

Having thus described my invention, I claim as new and desire to secure by Letters Patent—

1. The grooved cylinder K $k^1\,k^2$, in combination with a guide-pin, H, for controlling the line of fire and the sweep of the gun, substantially as herein shown and described.

145,563

2. The combination of an adjustable socket, G, guide-pin H, and grooved cylinder K k^1 k^2, for changing the sweep and line of fire of the gun, substantially as herein shown and described.

3. The flanged, grooved, perforated, and slotted cylinder or bar A, and the adjustable socket G, provided with a nut, F, in combination with the screw D, guide-pin H, and grooved cylinder K k^1 k^2, substantially as herein shown and described, and for the purpose set forth.

RICHARD J. GATLING.

Witnesses:
  EDGAR T. WELLES,
  DAVID L. ABERDEIN.

R. J. GATLING.
Traversing Mechanisms for Machine-Guns.

No. 145,563.   Patented Dec. 16, 1873.

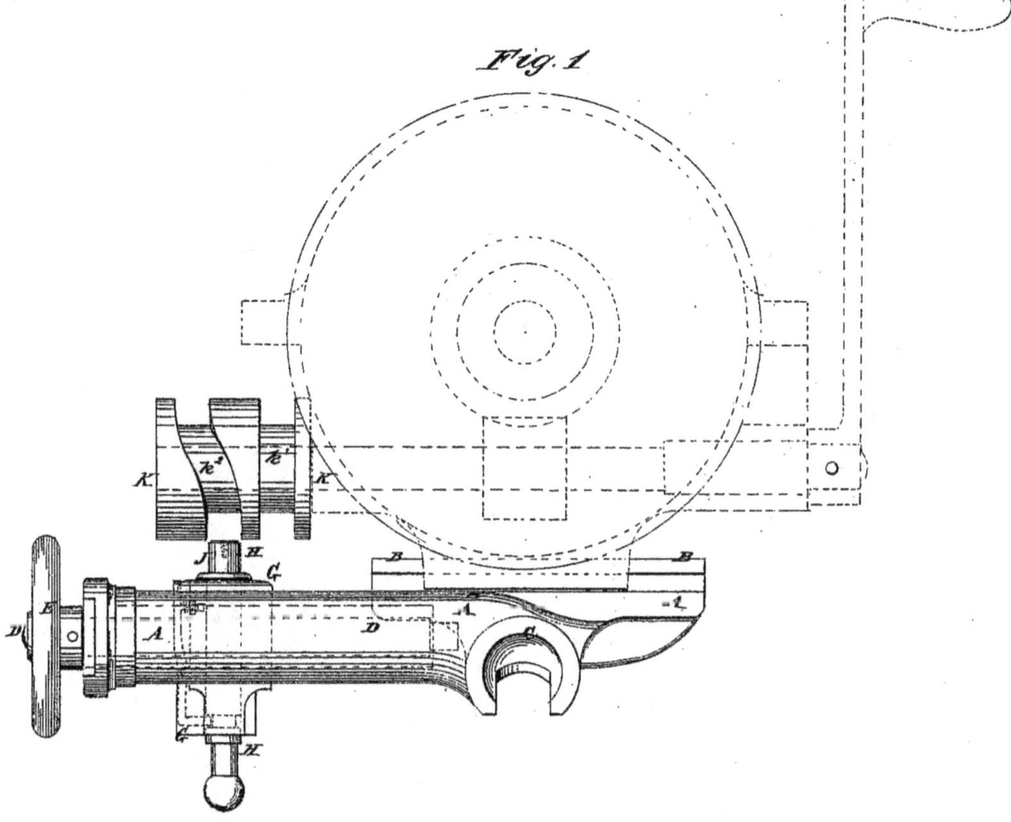

Fig. 1

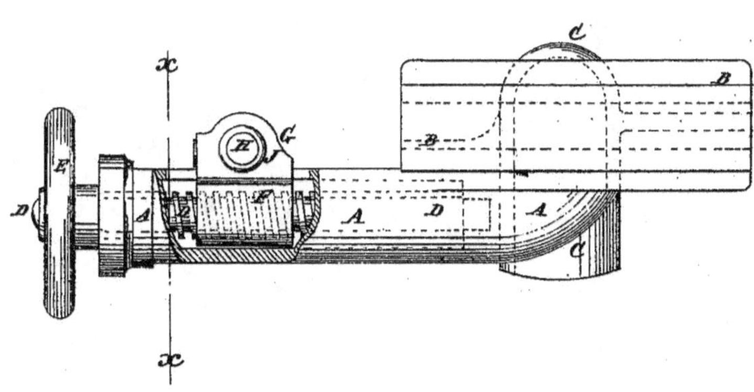

Fig. 2

WITNESSES:
A. W. Almqvist
C. Sedgwick

INVENTOR:
R. J. Gatling
BY
ATTORNEYS.

R. J. GATLING.
Traversing Mechanisms for Machine-Guns.

No. 145,563. Patented Dec. 16, 1873.

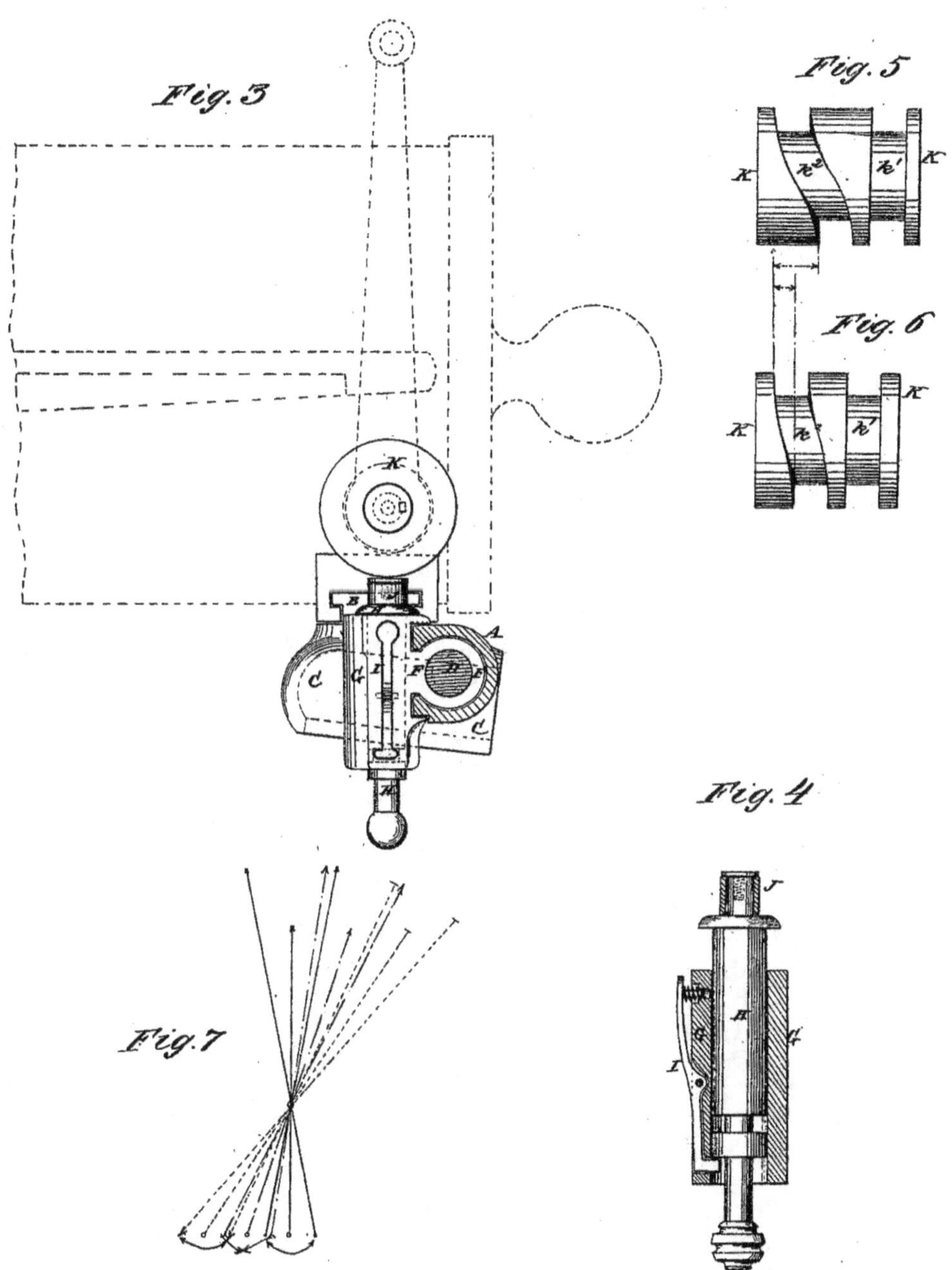

WITNESSES:
N. W. Almqvist
C. Sedgwick

INVENTOR:
R. J. Gatling

BY

ATTORNEYS.

UNITED STATES PATENT OFFICE.

RICHARD J. GATLING, OF HARTFORD, CONNECTICUT.

MACHINE-GUN

SPECIFICATION forming part of Letters Patent No. 497,781, dated May 23, 1893.

Application filed May 7, 1892. Serial No. 432,146. (No model.)

To all whom it may concern:

Be it known that I, RICHARD J. GATLING, a citizen of the United States, residing at Hartford, in the county of Hartford and State of Connecticut, have invented certain new and useful Improvements in Machine-Guns, of which the following is a full, clear, and exact specification.

The invention relates to the class of machine or battery guns known as Gatling guns, in which the barrels and locks are grouped about a central shaft around which they revolve in loading and firing, the object being to provide such a gun with a simple ejecting mechanism for aiding the extractors in removing the exploded cartridges, insuring a better extraction and increasing the efficiency and durability of the lock and extractor, and also to provide a simple means for admitting and holding a cooling liquid in the casing for preventing overheating of the barrels during action.

Referring to the accompanying drawings, where the invention is illustrated as applied to a gun of this class having ten barrels:—Figure 1 is a side view of the gun with a part cut in central vertical section to show the construction. Fig. 2 is a central vertical longitudinal section on an enlarged scale, of the butt of the gun. Fig. 3 is an end view with the cascabel plate removed. Fig. 4 is a cross-sectional view at the rear barrel plate, with a portion of the flanged disk which covers it, broken away. Fig. 5 is a side view of the lock. Fig. 6 is a top view. Fig. 7 is a sectional view of the same. Fig. 8 is a detail view of a portion of the edge of the rear barrel plate, showing an ejector. Fig. 9 is a detail sectional view of the rear end of a barrel and a portion of the rear plate showing a modified form of ejector. Fig. 10 is a face view of the same; and Fig. 11 is a perspective view of the latter form of ejector.

In the views 1 indicates the casing which is a metallic cylinder having any common means of attaching it to the mount or carriage, and the usual opening 2 for the reception of the ordinary cartridge feed case. A shaft 3 having at the butt the operating crank, passes through the cascabel plate 4, and is keyed to the barrel plates 5 and 6 which rotate freely in the casing. The front plate 5 is preferably formed of two disks secured together by rivets or screws with a ring 7 placed loosely in a groove in the periphery to reduce friction, while the rear plate is preferably formed of a disk 8, and a steel ring 9 held thereto by screws 10.

The barrels 11 which pass through the front plate and are firmly secured to the rear plate preferably have projecting lugs 12 at the breech back of the rear plate, in which are cut mortises 13 for the entrance of the extractors. The breeches of the barrels are chambered for the reception of the cartridges, and adjacent to these ends of the barrels are placed ejectors 14 which are preferably hung on pivots 15 supported in blocks 16 inserted into mortises 17 cut in the edge of the rear plate. These ejectors have shoulders 18 that project into the cartridge chambers and oscillate in the path of the cartridges so as to lie in front of their heads when the cartridges are loaded in the bore, and attached to the casing near the bottom in the path of these ejectors, so as to make contact with and oscillate them as they revolve with the rear plate, is a pin, wedge, or roll, 19.

The blocks 16 are preferably U-shaped, as shown in Fig. 8, with flanges to prevent them from rising out of the mortises when in motion, while back of them with a flange projecting over the edge of the rear plate, is secured a disk or cap 20.

Keyed to the shaft so as to rotate with it back of the rear plate is the cylinder 21 having the cartridge carriers 22 that revolve beneath the loading opening, and the grooves 23 in which reciprocate the breech plugs and locks 24 formed of blocks of suitable metal having their sides shaped to fit nicely and slide freely in the grooves.

The locks are provided with lugs 25 at one end that project into the groove in the cam cylinder 26 in such manner that the locks are reciprocated by the lugs and cam as they revolve. In perforations through the locks are the firing pins 27 normally thrust forward by coiled main springs, and in mortises along one edge of these locks are the extractors 28 which are slotted and move a short distance independently of the locks upon pins or rollers 29 with their spring tails or rear ends 30 resting upon pins or rollers 31. The front ends of the extractors are provided with hooks for engaging the rims of the cartridges, and they are thrust forward by springs so that normally the tenons 32 are at the forward ends of the mortises 33 in the lock. When the cam has pushed the locks, during their rotation, way forward, the ends of the extractors pass into and fill up the mortises 13 in the lugs 12, and, abutting against the ends of the barrels, are so pressed backward that the tenons 32 are at the rear ends of the mortises 33, while the ends of the locks which form the breech plugs, fill the openings in the cap 20 at the rear of the barrels and back up the cartridges.

The cam cylinder 26 supports on the interior near the bottom, post to which is attached the cocking switch 34 (Fig. 3) the circular groove of which catches and holds for a short time as they revolve, the flanged heads of the firing pins so that the main springs are compressed as the locks move forward to enable them to throw the firing pins violently forward when the heads reach and drop out of the end of the groove of the switch as in the gun in common use. The cam cylinder is made thicker or provided with a recoil plate 35 near the bottom where the cartridges are exploded, to receive the concussion of the locks at the discharge.

When the crank and shaft are rotated and the barrels and locks revolve to fire the gun, the cam thrusts each lock in succession closely against the cartridge as it is being fired, the extractor being forced to the backward limit of its movement in the lock by contact with the end of the barrel, and when the cam commences to pull back the lock after firing, the extractor does not at once move, but is thrust forward by its spring as the lock retreats, until the tenon 32 reaches the front end of the mortise 33. Then of course the extractor retreats with the lock and withdraws the exploded cartridge which has been started from the chamber by the ejector of the barrel in which the cartridge is fired. The roll 19 is so located in its attachment to the casing that after the cartridge is fired, between the time the lock commences its return movement and the time when the extractor begins to retreat, the edge of the ejector 14 in its rotation rides up on the edge of the roll and is oscillated so that it starts the cartridge from its chamber, and then the retreating extractor readily pulls the loosened shell from the chamber so that it may be expelled from the gun.

In the form shown in Figs. 9, 10, and 11 the ejectors 36 are formed to slide in the mortises in the edge of the rear barrel plate, instead of oscillating therein, although the oscillating form is preferred, as the oscillating ejector always fills its opening in the end of the barrel. These ejectors 36 are shaped at one end to conform to about one-half of the end of the barrel, and they are thrown forward to position by the cartridges as they are thrust into the bore and forced backward as they rotate with the rear barrel plate by a

roll, wedge or block 37 secured to one side of the casing, so as to start the cartridges before the extractors begin to pull.

A cylindrical shell 38 is held at one end tightly in a groove in the rear barrel plate, and at the front end by a flange 39 on the front plate so as to surround the barrels and revolve with them, and a portion of the shaft 3 is bored and provided with openings that lead from the bore to the interior of the shell. The front end of the shaft is threaded and provided with a cap or nut 40 which can be removed at any time so that water or any other cooling liquid may be poured into the shell through the shaft to keep down the temperature of the barrels during action.

An ordinary feed case with cartridges is placed above the opening through the casing and as the shaft is rotated the carriers draw the cartridges into the gun. As the barrels and locks revolve the cam at the butt reciprocates the locks causing them to successively and continuously feed, load and fire the live cartridges and extract the ejected exploded shells.

When the gun is provided with the ejectors described, the discharged shells which are usually swollen and expanded by the explosion and tightly fit the chamber in the bore, will be started by the action of a powerful and strong little ejector which can be constructed so wide as to preclude any possibility of pulling or tearing the heads off the shells which stick in the bore, and which ejectors act with but little additional friction. As the extractors do not have to start the cartridges from the bore they may be lighter and will last longer as but little power is required to remove the loosened shells, thus reducing the weight and also the momentum of the reciprocating locks.

With the construction shown for surrounding the barrels with a cooling liquid, the water jacket or shell as it revolves with the barrel plates and barrels may be permanently and tightly fitted in place so that the liquid cannot leak or evaporate, and at the same time the liquid may be readily poured in or drawn out from around the barrels.

I claim as my invention—

1. In combination in a machine gun having a group of barrels, movable ejectors located adjacent to each barrel, locks bearing extractors adapted to reciprocate toward and from each barrel, and a cam for reciprocating the locks, substantially as specified.

2. In combination in a machine gun having revolving barrels, movable ejectors located adjacent to each barrel, a projection attached to the casing in the path of revolution of the ejectors for moving them, and locks bearing extractors adapted to reciprocate toward and from the barrels, substantially as specified.

3. In combination in a machine gun having revolving barrels, locks and extractors, movable ejectors located adjacent to each barrel, and a projection attached to the casing in the

path of revolution of the ejectors for moving them, substantially as specified.

4. In combination in a machine gun, a revolving shaft supporting barrel-plates and a cylinder, barrels supported by the plates, ejectors located in mortises in the plates adjacent to the barrels, and reciprocating locks and extractors supported by the cylinder, substantially as specified.

5. In combination with the revolving barrels of a machine gun of the within described class, oscillating ejectors pivoted in sockets in the barrel plate adjacent to and movable with the breech of each barrel, substantially as specified.

6. In combination with the revolving barrels of a machine gun of the within described class, a lock consisting of a block bearing a spring firing pin, an extractor loosely pivoted to the block so as to have small independent longitudinal and oscillating movements, with a wide hooked portion on one side of the pivot and a narrow elastic portion on the opposite side of the pivot, and a spiral spring thrusting longitudinally against the extractor, the longitudinal movement of the extractor being controlled by the spiral spring, and the oscillating movement by the integral elastic portion, substantially as specified.

7. In combination with the revolving barrels of a machine gun of the within described class, a lock consisting of a block bearing a spring firing pin, and an extractor having a small reciprocating movement independent of the block supported on rollers journaled in mortises in the block, substantially as specified.

8. In a machine gun having a group of moving barrels, a central shaft for supporting such barrels, said shaft having a longitudinal perforation with openings leading to the interior of the casing, and a cap for closing the end of the perforation, substantially as specified.

RICHARD J. GATLING.

Witnesses:
   H. R. WILLIAMS,
   C. E. BUCKLAND.

R. J. GATLING
MACHINE GUN.

No. 497,781. Patented May 23, 1893.

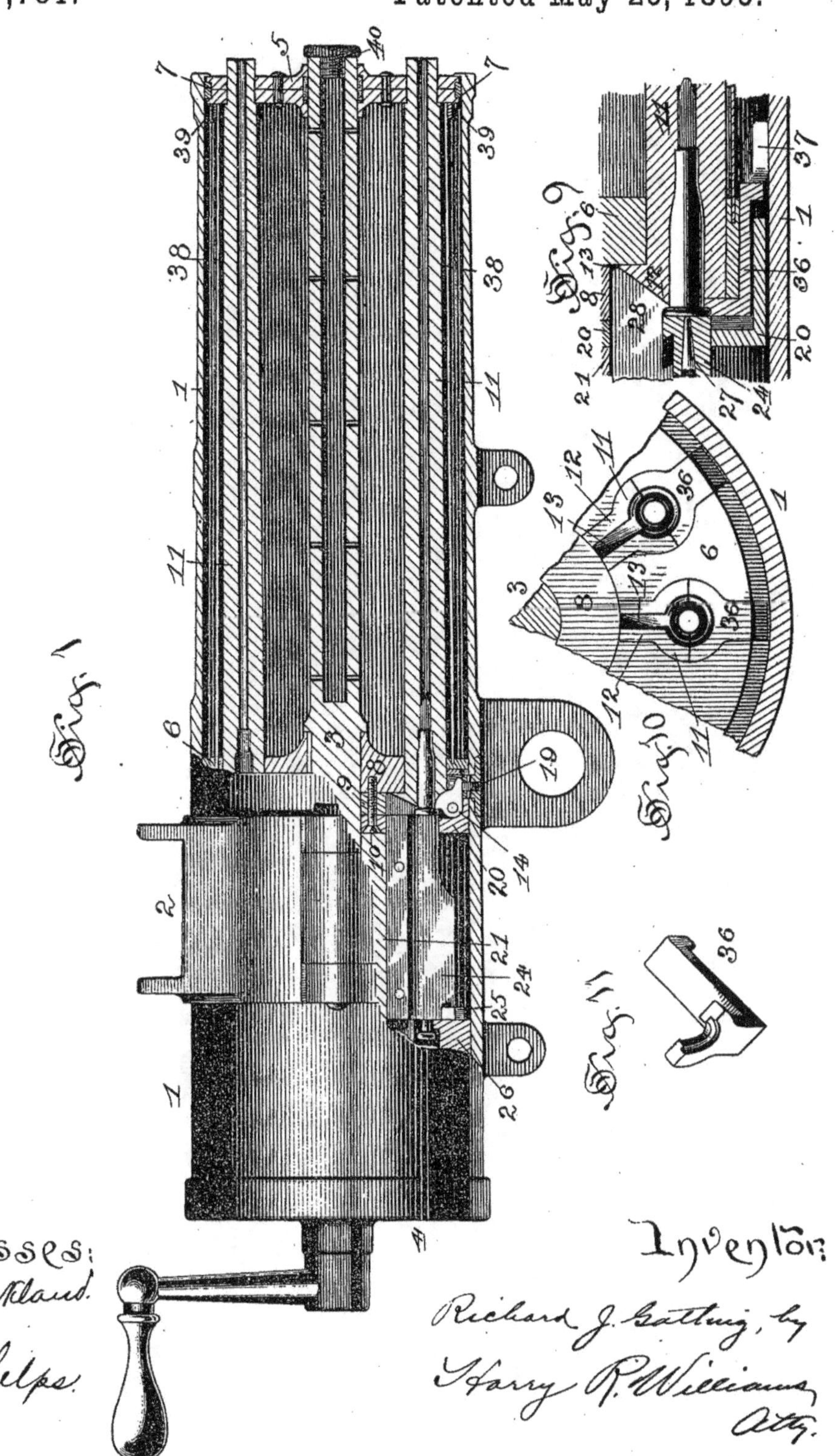

Witnesses:
C. E. Buckland.
D. A. Phelps.

Inventor:
Richard J. Gatling, by
Harry R. Williams
Atty.

R. J. GATLING.
MACHINE GUN.

No. 497,781.   Patented May 23, 1893

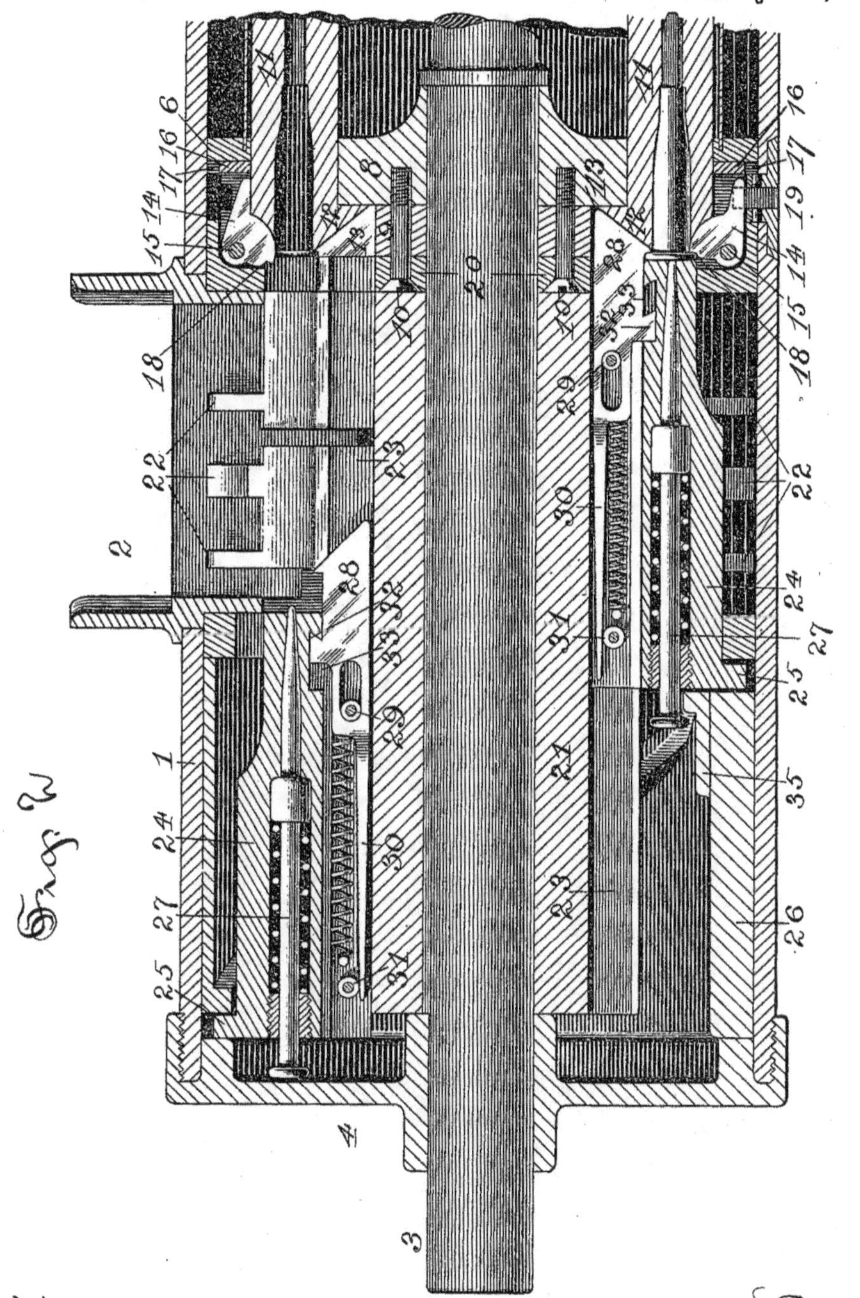

Witnesses:
C. E. Buckland,
P. A. Phelps.

Inventor:
Richard J. Gatling, by
Harry R. Williams,
Atty.

R. J. GATLING.
MACHINE GUN.

No. 497,781.   Patented May 23, 1893.

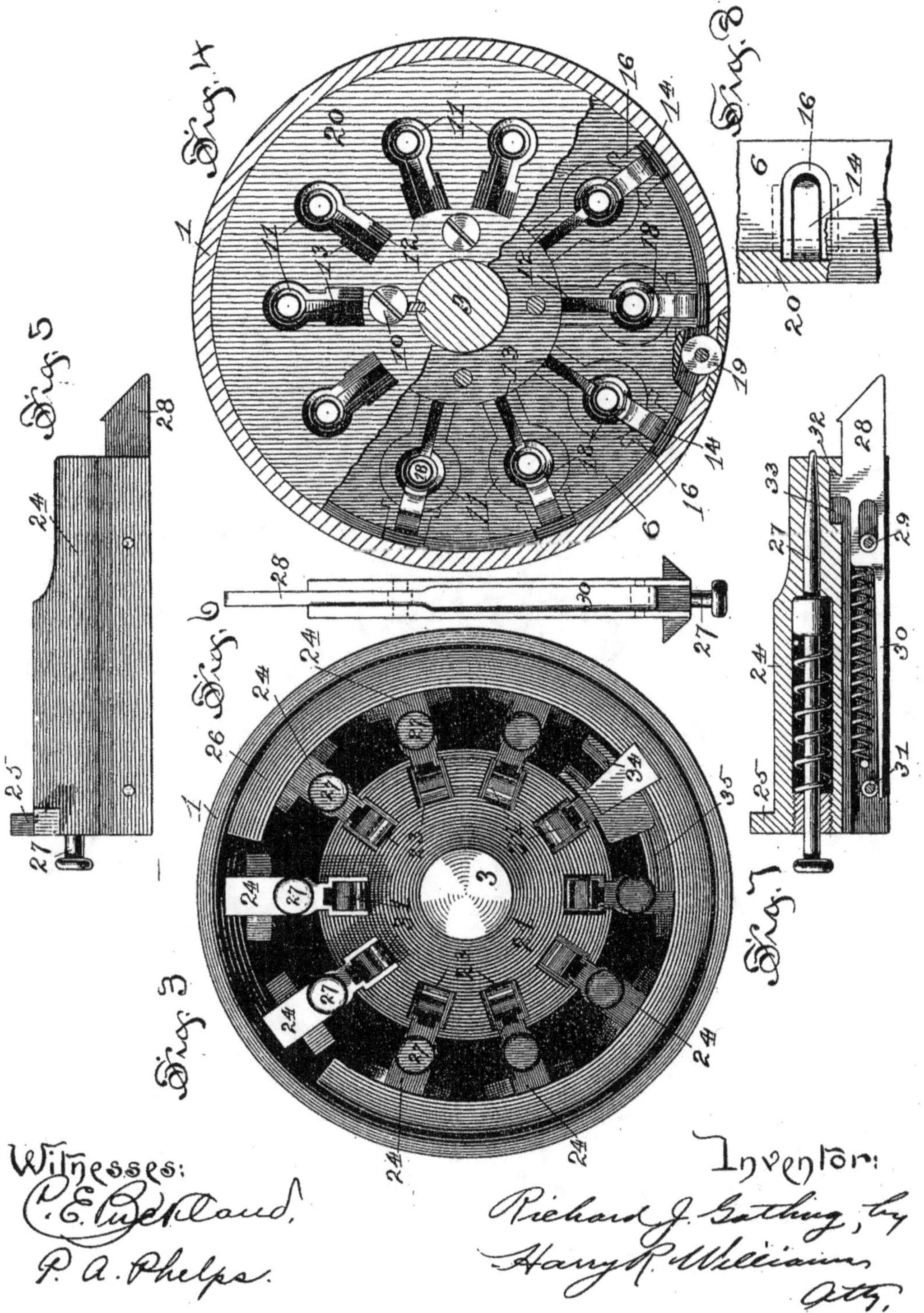

Witnesses:
C. E. Buckland.
P. A. Phelps.

Inventor:
Richard J. Gatling, by
Harry R. Williams
Atty.

United States Patent Office.

RICHARD J. GATLING, OF HARTFORD, CONNECTICUT.

FEED FOR MACHINE-GUNS.

SPECIFICATION forming part of Letters Patent No. 499,534, dated June 13, 1893.

Application filed July 22, 1892. Serial No. 440,880. (No model.)

To all whom it may concern:

Be it known that I, RICHARD J. GATLING, a citizen of the United States, residing at Hartford, in the county of Hartford and State of 5 Connecticut, have invented certain new and useful Improvements in Feeds for Machine-Guns, of which the following is a full, clear, and exact specification.

The invention relates to the devices provided 10 for feeding cartridges into the breech of machine-guns of that class known as Gatling guns, the object being to produce a simple and cheap feed into which a number of cartridges may be rapidly placed directly from 15 the package in which they are stored and transported, and quickly forced into the breech of the gun, whereby a number of cartridges can be discharged with great rapidity simulating volley firing.

20 Referring to the accompanying drawings: Figure 1. is a reduced plan of a Gatling-gun provided with the improvement. Fig. 2. is a transverse section through the revolving lock-cylinder and feed of such a gun. Fig. 25 3. is a plan of the hopper of the gun. Fig. 4. is an edge view of the same. Fig. 5. is a view looking into the hopper. Fig. 6. is a plan of the feed-case. Fig. 7. is an end view of the feed case. Fig. 8. is an edge view of the 30 same; and Fig. 9. is a detail vertical section of the feed gate.

In the views 1 indicates the frame; 2 the revolving barrels; and 3 the butt-casing in which, on the central shaft 4, is supported the 35 revolving lock-cylinder 5 which bears the reciprocating locks of a Gatling-gun of common form and construction.

Adjacent to the breech of the barrels in continuation of the casing is a hopper 6 which 40 is pivoted to one side of the frame and provided at the opposite side with a spring catch 7 whereby the hopper may be secured down to close, or thrown over to open the breech. An opening 8 is made through a portion of 45 this hopper and from the lower side of this opening projecting outward on an incline is a shelf 9 adapted to support the end of the feed-case which holds the cartridges. This feed-case consists of a plate 10 having along 50 the rear edge an upright flange, a portion of which, 11, is flat while a portion, 12, is provided with a mortise 13 adapted to receive and hold the heads of the cartridges. A rod 14 is secured along one side so as to extend the whole, or only a portion of the length of 55 the plate as desired, and hinged upon this rod so that it may turn over as well as slide back and forth, is a block 15 having a handle 16. The shelf 9 preferably projects outward quite a distance to afford a firm support for 60 the feed-case also that the case may be readily placed upon the shelf and slipped into the opening 8 in the dark. Around the upper side of the opening is a flange 17 mortised to receive and hold the flanged side of the feed- 65 case, while on the opposite side is a flange 18 mortised to receive and hold the flat edge of the feed-case, a flange 19 being formed to guide the cartridges into the gun as they pass down the feed-case. In a mortise in the top 70 of the hopper preferably in an adjustable block 20 is placed a fluted roll 21 adapted to act as a gate and separate the cartridges as they are fed into the gun so that but one at a time can pass into the cartridge receiving 75 cavity. This roll, in the construction shown, is supported upon a shaft 22 journaled in blocks 23 which are adjustably held in the block 20 by means of the screws 24. When the end of the feed-case is thrust into the 80 opening through the hopper and there held by means of the spring catch 25, the block 15 is turned over on the rod 14 to the position illustrated in dotted outline in Figs. 6 and 7 so that the upper surface of the plate is free 85 from obstruction. A number of cartridges in an original paper package or held by any other common means are placed on the plate with their heads against the flat flange 11 and as the package in this position is quickly 90 drawn down toward the gun the heads of the cartridges pass into the mortise 13, then the package is pulled off and thrown aside leaving the cartridges on the plate with their heads in the mortise. The block 15 is then 95 turned on its hinge to the position shown in full lines in the drawings and when the gun is in operation these cartridges are by a quick thrust on the handle of the block pushed into the gun and there rapidly fired in the ordi- 10 nary manner. The plate 10 may be made of any convenient length to receive any number of cartridges, and the flange 11 may be made of suitable height so that the heads of the cartridges may be properly guided into the mortise 13 without special skill, ready to be forced into the gun.   With this method of feeding the cartridges are pushed into the gun in groups during action very quickly, each group being fired rapidly as a volley with much greater rapidity than if fed in with a regular steady feed.   This is of great utility in ordinary action but is of especial advantage when the gun is operated by means of a motor, for the reason that the mechanism of the gun can be operated continuously by power while the cartridges need be only fired when desirable to accomplish the greatest effect, as in firing a volley from a boat when it is on the crest of a wave or when an enemy suddenly appears and disappears.

The feed is simple and cheap in construction, readily inserted in place in the gun and is so formed as to conveniently receive a number of cartridges directly from the original package without loss of time, so that volleys can be fired with great rapidity.

I claim as my invention—

1. A feed for machine guns, consisting of a plate having a flange with a mortised groove adapted to receive the heads of the cartridges, and a sliding block hinged to the plate and movable thereon through the groove for forcing the cartridges therefrom, substantially as specified.

2. A feed for machine guns, consisting of a plate having a flange with a mortised groove adapted to receive the heads of the cartridges, a flange adapted to guide the heads of the cartridges into the groove, and a sliding block movable on said plate through the groove for forcing the cartridges therefrom, substantially as specified.

3. A feed for machine guns, consisting of a plate having a flange with a mortised groove adapted to receive the heads of the cartridges, a flange adapted to guide the heads of the cartridges into the groove, a rod secured to the side of the plate, and a sliding block pivoted upon said rod for forcing the cartridges from the groove, substantially as specified.

RICHARD J. GATLING.

Witnesses:
   H. R. WILLIAMS,
   C. E. BUCKLAND.

R. J. GATLING.
FEED FOR MACHINE GUNS.

No. 499,534.   Patented June 13, 1893.

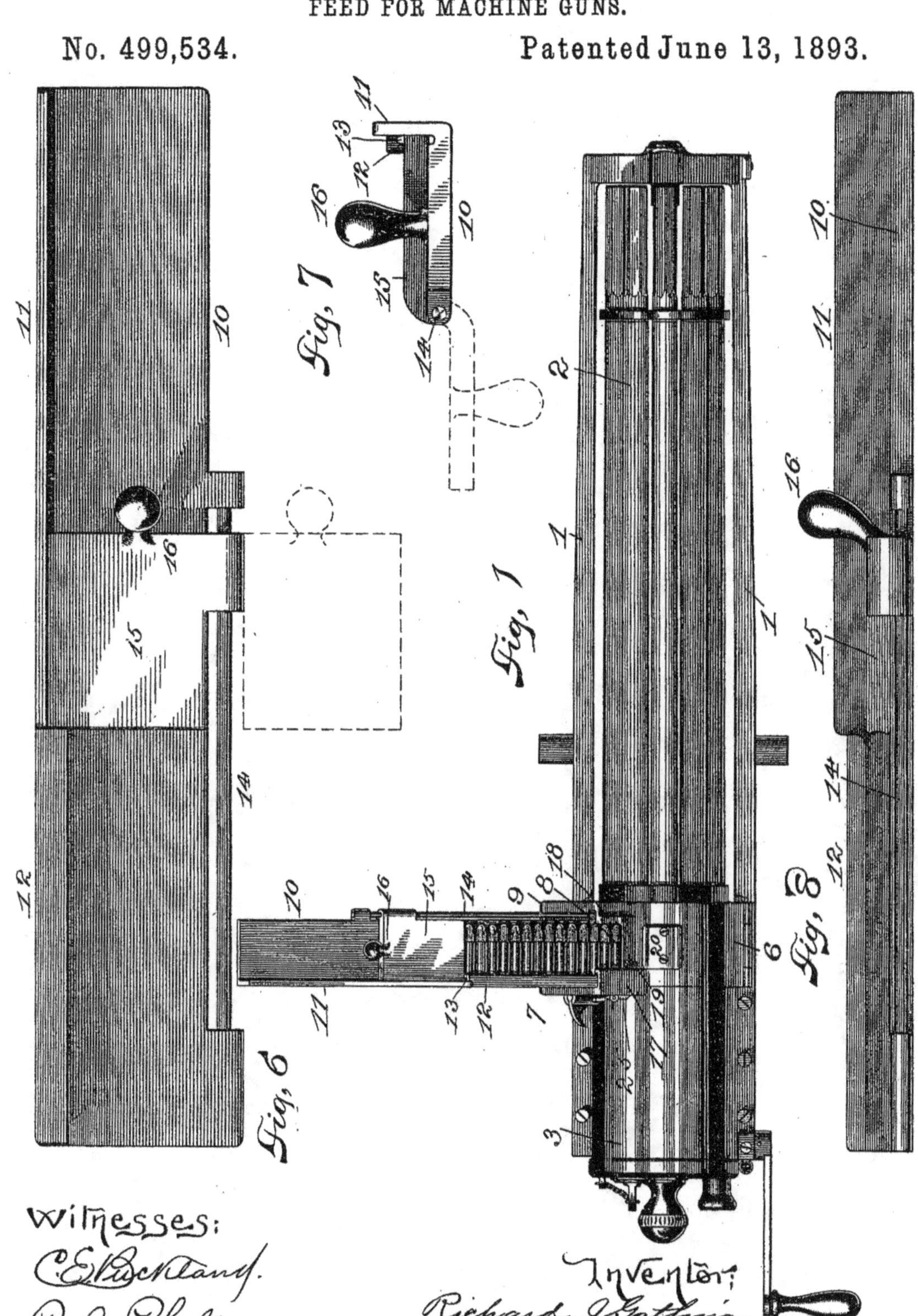

Witnesses:
C. E. Buckland,
P. A. Phelps,

Inventor:
Richard J. Gatling,
Harry R. Williams,
by att.

R. J. GATLING.
FEED FOR MACHINE GUNS.

No. 499,534.						Patented June 13, 1893.

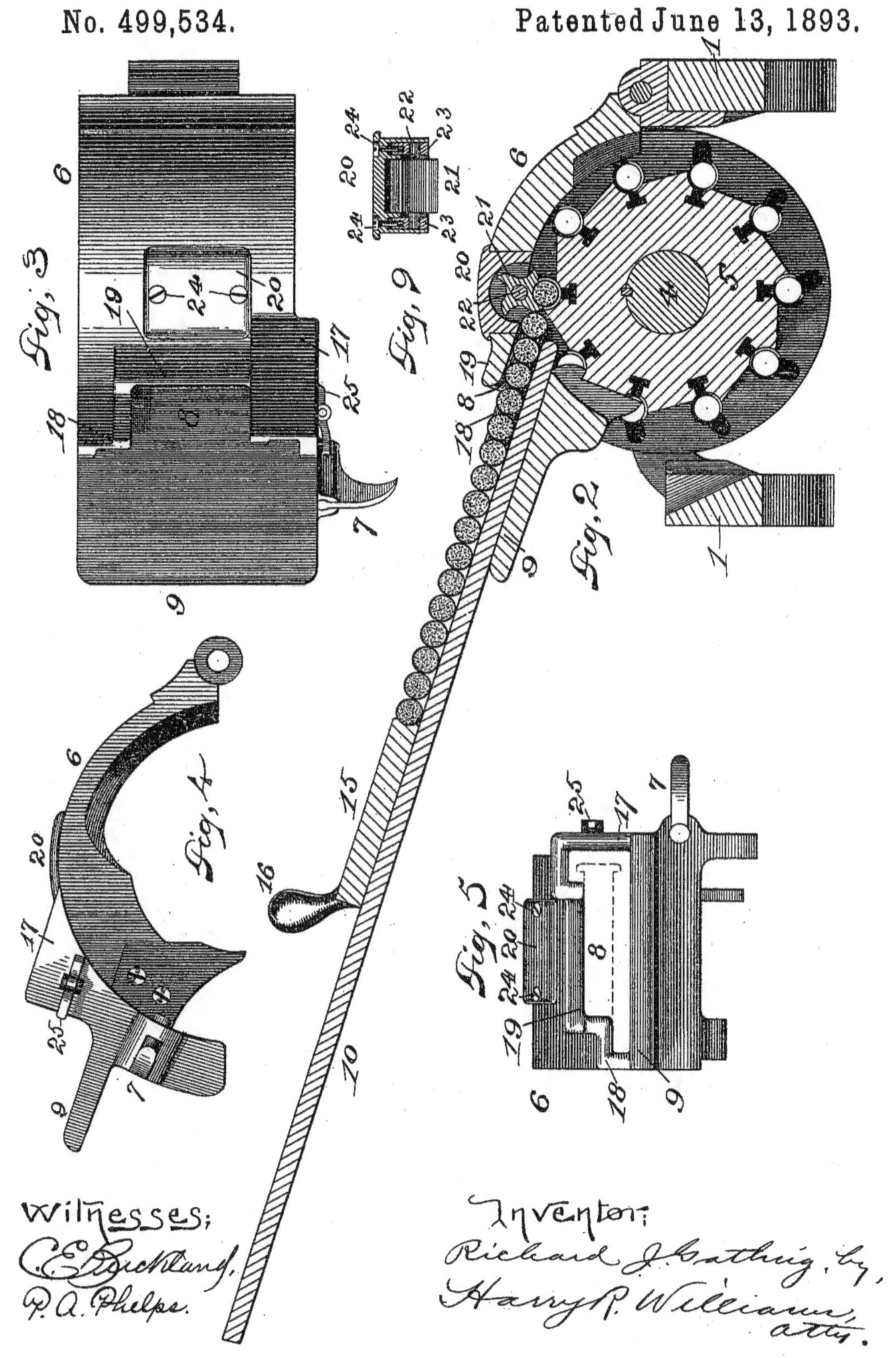

Witnesses:
C. E. Buckland.
P. A. Phelps.

Inventor:
Richard J. Gatling, by,
Harry R. Williams,
atty.

RICHARD J. GATLING, OF HARTFORD, CONNECTICUT.

MACHINE-GUN.

SPECIFICATION forming part of Letters Patent No. 502,185, dated July 25, 1893.

Application filed September 10, 1892. Serial No. 445,492. (No model.)

To all whom it may concern:

Be it known that I, RICHARD J. GATLING, a citizen of the United States, residing at Hartford, in the county of Hartford and State of Connecticut, have invented certain new and useful Improvements in Machine-Guns, of which the following is a full, clear, and exact specification.

The invention relates to the class of machine guns commonly known as Gatling guns, the object being to provide a gun of this class which can be readily changed so as to be fired with great rapidity either by hand or by power, the power driving mechanism being so constructed that it may be quickly removed, or attached in such manner that it is out of sight and not a mark for hostile projectiles or in the way of the gunners; and further to so construct the mechanism of the gun that the parts may be quickly removed and assembled, and enable cartridges of small caliber to be used and positively extracted after being fired.

To this end the invention resides in a gun having a frame or casing supporting a cylindrical cam and a central revolving shaft bearing coils of wire, a group of barrels and a cylinder with reciprocating locks, and in details of the construction of these parts, as more particularly hereinafter described and pointed out in the claims.

Referring to the accompanying drawings:— Figure 1 is a side view of one of these guns of the class known as the "army gun." Fig. 2 is a plan of the same. Fig. 3 is a side view of one of these guns of the class known as the "navy gun." Fig. 4 is a plan of this latter gun. Fig. 5 is a plan of the revolving parts of one of the guns. Fig. 6 is an enlarged central longitudinal vertical section of the butt of the gun shown in Fig. 1. Fig. 7 is a section on plane denoted by the broken line a a. Fig. 8 is a section on plane denoted by b b. Fig. 9 is a section on plane c c. Fig. 10 is a section on d d. Fig. 11 is a view of the breech of the barrels and their holder. Fig. 12 is a section of a portion of the same. Fig. 13 is a section of the cam cylinder; and Fig. 14 shows top, bottom, side, sectional and end views of one of the locks.

In the views 1 indicates the trunnion frame which consists of a pair of metallic bars connected together at their front ends by a cross-piece 2, and at their rear ends by the casing 3. This cylindrical casing 3 is divided diametrically and the upper part hinged to the lower so that it may be thrown open to expose the interior when its catch is released and the casing 4, that is screwed upon a mutilated thread on the end of this casing, is removed. A shaft 5 passing through the center from end to end of the gun is supported at the front by the cross-piece of the frame and at the rear end by the cascabel plate or a bearing in the cascabel. It is preferred that this shaft be formed in two sections joined back of the casing 3 by means of a coupling 6 so that the rear portion of the shaft may be separated from the forward portion and removed. Keyed to the shaft are the barrel disks, the front disk, 7, being perforated and holding the barrels near their muzzles, while the rear disk, 8, is perforated and holds the butts of the barrels which are provided with lugs 9. The disk 8 is chambered and in the chamber is placed a disk 10 of hard steel, having a number of mortises in its periphery to receive and hold the lugs projecting from the ends of the barrels, so that the barrels are prevented from twisting or turning under the strain of the bullets as they pass through the rifling. The lock carrier cylinder 11 is keyed to the shaft directly back of this disk 10 so as to hold the disk in place, and in grooves in this cylinder slide the locks 12 as they are reciprocated by the cam cut in the interior of the cylinder 13 that fits into the casing 3 which has a socket to receive a pin 14 that projects from the cylinder so as to insure the correct location of the parts.

Each of the locks 12 consists of a block 15 which forms a breech block, having a tongue 16 that runs in a groove in the carrier block and a lug 17 that fits the cam groove so that the locks are reciprocated by the cam as the carrier revolves with the locks as in the common Gatling gun. In a central perforation through each lock-block is placed a spring firing pin 18 having a head 19 adapted to engage the cocking switch 20 located on the interior of the cam cylinder back of the recoil block 40, as in the common construction, while in a longitudinal mortise in the top of the block is an extractor 21, having a hooked forward end adapted to engage the upper portion of the rim of a cartridge, and in a mortise in the bottom of this block is an extractor 22 having a hooked end adapted to engage the lower part of the rim of the cartridge to withdraw it from the barrel after it has been fired. The extractor 21 is formed of a piece of spring steel, and has a small reciprocation in the mortise on its holding pin, while the extractor 22 has a longitudinal movement on its holding pin, and is thrust forward by means of the spring 23, the elastic tail of this extractor riding on a roll in the bottom of the mortise.

A diaphragm 24 with a bearing for the center shaft is located in the rear of the casing 3 behind the cam cylinder, and this diaphragm is divided, the upper part 25 being hinged to the lower so that it may be lifted when the top of the casing is lifted, to allow a free removal of the locks from the grooves in the carrier block.

In the construction shown, to the central shaft 5 is keyed a core 26 of magnetic material with a common winding of wire 27 forming an armature of an electric motor which when electrically excited rotates the shaft, while loosely mounted upon the shaft is a frame 28 which bears an electro field magnet 29. To the frame 28 of this field magnet is secured a gear 30 that meshes into gears 31 secured to shafts 32 which are journaled in the ends of a coupling 33 and which bear gears 34 in mesh with a gear 35 secured to a diaphragm 36 extending across the forward end of this casing. The coupling 33 is removably secured to the end of the shaft of the gun where the usual crank-handle would be attached, and also to the extension of the shaft which bears the armature of the electric motor.

The field magnet is wound in the customary manner and connected with its source of excitation in any common manner, and the armature is also wound as usual and connected in the ordinary way with any suitable source of electrical supply.

To start the gun into action the motor is excited by a current of electricity. The construction and arrangement described are such that the armature revolves in one direction, and being connected with the main shaft revolves it and operates the gun, while through the medium of the intermeshing gears the field revolves in an opposite direction in order that the revolutions of the armature may be slower so that the speed of the firing may be better regulated.

At the forward end of the casing 3 in the frame of the gun shown and described in Figs. 1 and 2, a hopper 37 made of a form to receive a cartridge feed slide of the class known as the "Bruce feed," is hinged to the frame on one side and provided with a catch on the opposite side to permit of its being opened or closed. Formed on or secured to the under side of this hopper are the plows 38 (Figs. 6 and 10) which extend into the path of the exploded cartridge shells after they have been extracted from the barrels, to eject them from the gun, as in the Gatling gun in common use.

In the form of gun shown in Figs. 3 and 4, the barrels are surrounded by a shell 39 for nearly their entire length, and in this shell water or any suitable cooling liquid may be placed to keep down the temperature of the barrels. In this form the upper part of the rear end of the casing and the hopper are hinged to a portion of the shell, the hopper shown in this connection being that of common form which is designed to receive the ordinary "drum feed" used with guns of this class.

I claim as my invention—

1. In combination with the frame of a machine gun, a revolving shaft bearing an armature a group of barrels and a mortised cylinder holding reciprocating locks, a casing inclosing a field magnet adjacent to the armature, and a cylindrical cam in the path of the locks, substantially as specified.

2. In combination with the frame of a machine gun, a revolving shaft bearing an armature a group of barrels and a mortised cylinder holding reciprocating locks, a casing supporting a cylindrical cam in the path of the locks, and a casing detachably secured to the former casing and inclosing a field magnet adjacent to the armature, substantially as specified.

3. In combination with the frame of a machine gun, a revolving shaft bearing a group of barrels and a mortised cylinder holding reciprocating locks, a sectional hinged casing supporting a cylindrical cam in the path of the locks, a hopper hinged to the frame adjacent to the breech of the barrels, and means for revolving the shaft, substantially as specified.

4. In combination with the frame of a machine gun, a revolving shaft bearing a group of barrels and a mortised cylinder holding reciprocating locks, a sectional hinged casing supporting a cylindrical-cam in the path of the locks, a sectional hinged diaphragm at the rear of said casing, a hopper hinged to the frame adjacent to the breech of the barrels, and means for revolving the shaft, substantially as specified.

5. In combination with the frame of a machine gun, a revolving shaft bearing a mortised cylinder holding reciprocating locks, and disks holding a group of barrels, the rear one of said disks being formed of a portion with circular perforations and a portion of harder metal having mortises adjacent to the circular perforations, barrels with lugs projecting from their rear ends into said mortises, a casing supporting a cylindrical cam in the path of the locks, and means for revolving the shaft, substantially as specified.

RICHARD J. GATLING.

Witnesses:
  H. R. WILLIAMS,
  CLARENCE E. BUCKLAND.

R. J. GATLING.
MACHINE GUN.

No. 502,185.   Patented July 25, 1893.

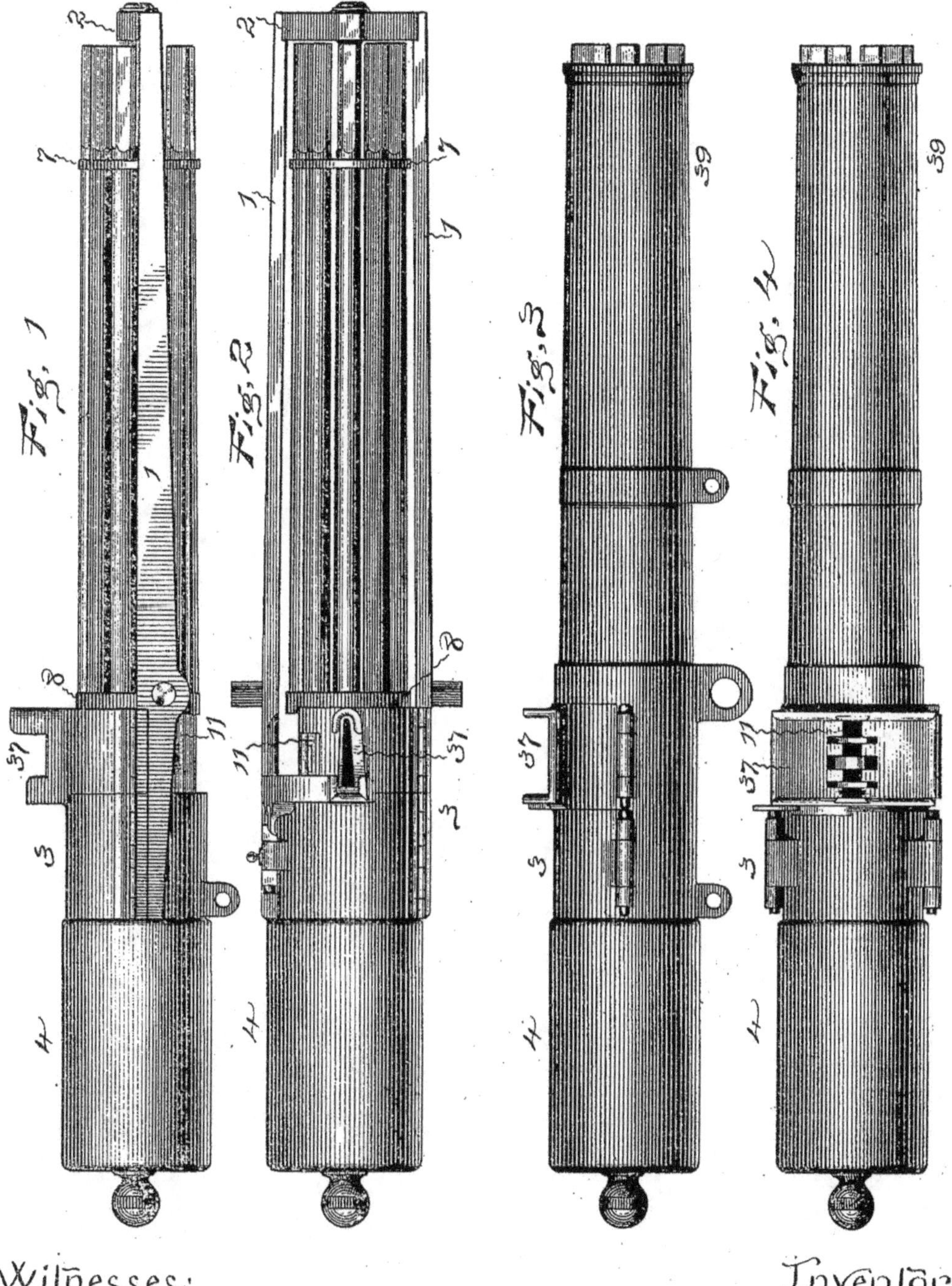

Witnesses: Inventor;
Clarence E. Buckland.   Richard J. Gatling by,
R. A. Phelps.   Harry P. Williams,
                                              Atty.

R. J. GATLING.
MACHINE GUN.

No. 502,185.   Patented July 25, 1893.

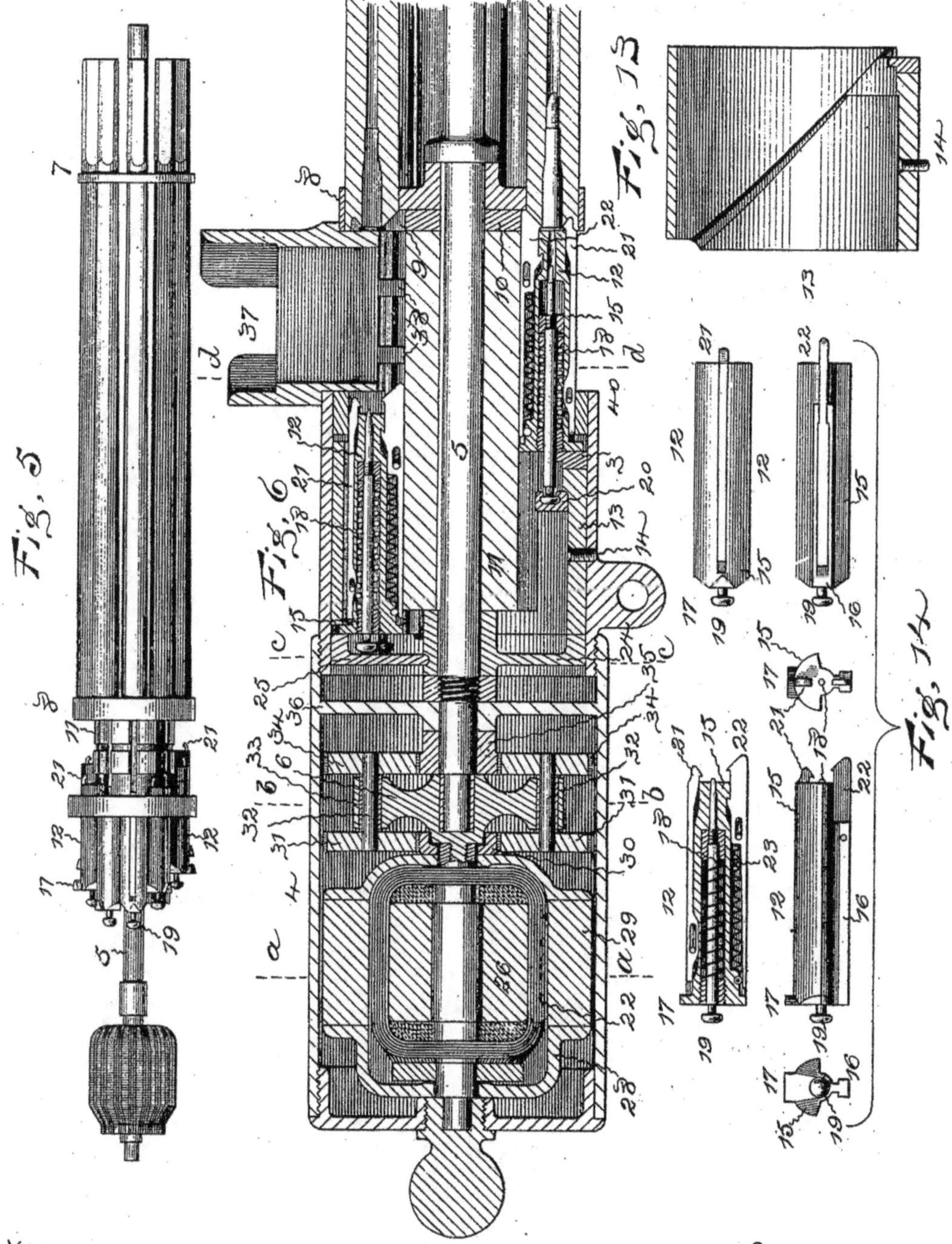

Witnesses:
Clarence E. Buckland.
P. A. Phelps.

Inventor:
Richard J. Gatling by
Harry R. Williams
Atty.

R. J. GATLING.
MACHINE GUN.

No. 502,185.   Patented July 25, 1893.

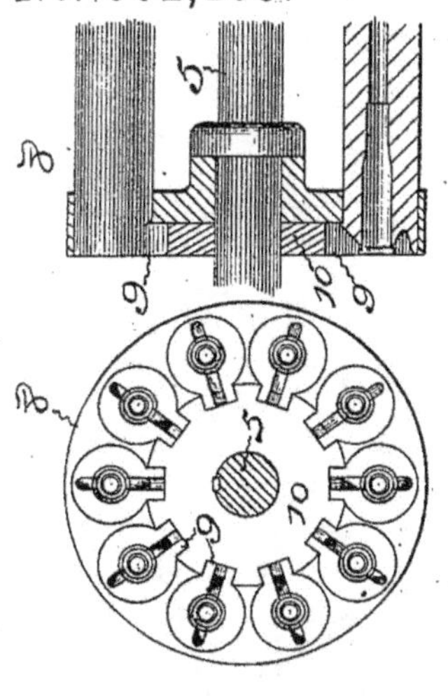

Fig. 11

Fig. 12

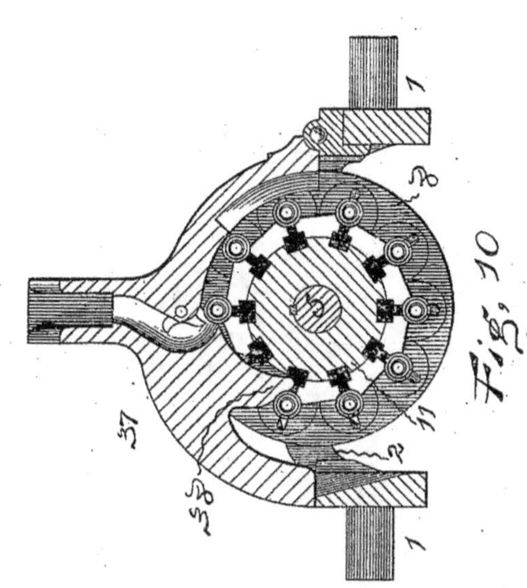

Fig. 10

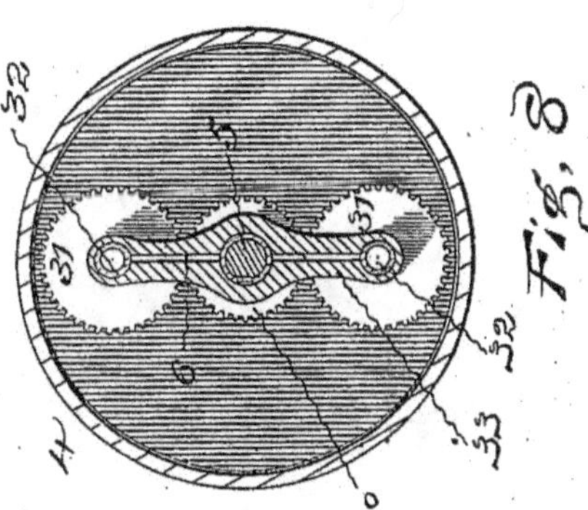

Fig. 8

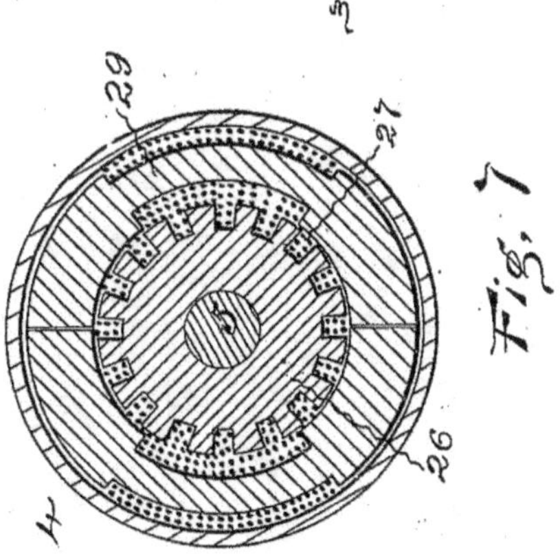

Fig. 7

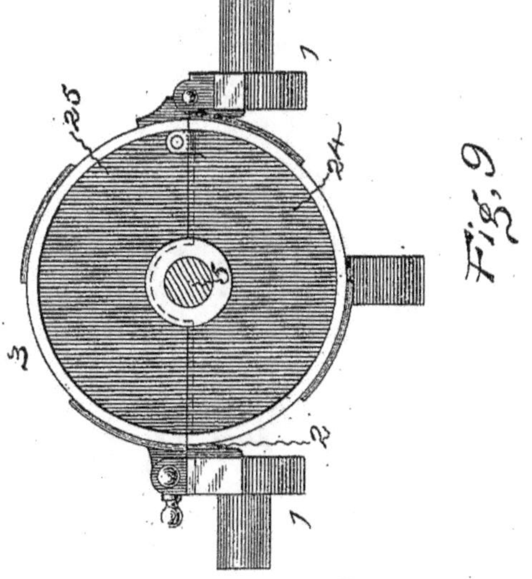

Fig. 9

Witnesses:
Clarence E. Buckland.
P. A. Phelps.

Inventor:
Richard J. Gatling, by
Harry R. Williams,
atty.

United States Patent Office.

RICHARD J. GATLING, OF HARTFORD, CONNECTICUT.

FEED FOR MAGAZINE-GUNS.

SPECIFICATION forming part of Letters Patent No. 502,882, dated August 8, 1893.

Application filed October 15, 1892. Serial No. 448,967. (No model.)

To all whom it may concern:

Be it known that I, RICHARD J. GATLING, a citizen of the United States, residing at Hartford, in the county of Hartford and State of Connecticut, have invented certain new and useful Improvements in Feeds for Machine-Guns, of which the following is a full, clear, and exact specification.

The invention relates to that class of devices known as gravity feeds provided for feeding cartridges to Gatling guns, and the object of the invention is to provide a simple, convenient and cheap arrangement which will insure the certain passage of the cartridges, without catching, sticking or clogging, from a gravity feed into the gun.

To this end the invention resides in a feed plate, that can be quickly inserted into or removed from the hopper of the gun, having a groove for receiving the heads of the cartridges, and vibrating slides to prevent the cartridges from catching and holding in the groove so that they will rapidly slide into the gun, with a device for reciprocating the slides, as more particularly hereinafter described and pointed out in the claims.

Referring to the accompanying drawings:— Figure 1 is a plan view of a Gatling gun provided with the improved feed. Fig. 2 is an enlarged vertical transverse section through the hopper and gun just back of the feed plate. Fig. 3 is a front view of the feed plate. Fig. 4 is a vertical section of the same. Fig. 5 is a detail cross-section on planes *a*, *b*, and *c*; and Fig. 6 is a detail view of one of the slides.

In the views 1 indicates the frame of a Gatling gun of ordinary form and construction, having the usual breech casing 2, group of rotary barrels 3, and crank 4 for revolving the barrels. At the rear of the barrels just forward of the breech casing, is the customary hopper 5 which being hinged to one side of the frame and provided with a catch at the other side, may be lifted up to uncover the breech of the barrels as in the ordinary Gatling gun. This hopper has an opening through the top for the passage of cartridges, and at the rear of this opening is a rectangular pocket 6 adapted to receive and hold the lower end of the feed. This feed consists of a plate 7 having a flange along one edge for about its entire length, and a flange at the opposite edge for only a portion of its length. These flanges form a groove to receive the heads of the cartridges which while in the original package are put up to the upper end of the long flange against the plate and drawn downward until the heads pass into the groove between the flanges and are there held so that the package can be removed and thrown away. Both of these flanges in the form shown are mortised, preferably with an under cut on the inside, and in these mortises are placed slides 8 that are free to be reciprocated vertically. Connected with these slides by pins 9 is a lever 10 having downward projecting arms, pivoted to the lower end of the plate in such manner that when the feed is thrust into the pocket in the hopper and there held by means of a set-screw 11, the ends of this lever will come in contact with the periphery of a portion of the lock-carrying cylinder 12 that is keyed to the central shaft of the gun. The periphery of this cylinder, common to all the prior Gatling guns, is indented, serrated or fluted, so that when it is rotated in firing the gun, the lever will be oscillated. This oscillation of the lever causes the slides to which it is connected, to be alternately reciprocated, and as the slides form the side walls of the groove which holds the heads of the cartridges, any tendency of those heads to clog, catch or stick in the grooves is obviated, and any dust or dirt which collects in the groove is shaken out by this alternate reciprocation or vibration of the slides forming the side walls of the groove and at the same time the heads of the cartridges are shaken down, so that by this simple, cheap and convenient means cartridges may be held merely by the heads, and fed by gravity into the gun with great rapidity without any danger of catching, sticking, or clogging so as to interfere with the rapid firing of the gun.

Of course but one side of the groove may be made with a vibrating slide, if desired, while the construction is equally applicable to the ordinary gravity feed having the double groove for reciprocating two rows of cartridges instead of one.

I claim as my invention—

1. A feed for machine guns, consisting of a grooved plate for receiving cartridges set into an opening in a gun, and a slide held by the plate adjacent to the cartridge groove and re-

ciprocated longitudinally by the revolution of the gun when in action, substantially as specified.

2. A feed for machine guns, consisting of a grooved plate for receiving cartridges set into an opening in a gun, and slides supported by the plate on each side of the cartridge groove reciprocated longitudinally by the revolution of the gun when in action, substantially as specified.

3. A feed for machine guns, consisting of a grooved plate for receiving cartridges, a slide supported by the plate adjacent to the cartridge groove, and a lever connected with the slide and reciprocated longitudinally by the revolution of the gun when in action, substantially as specified.

4. A feed for machine guns, consisting of a grooved plate for receiving cartridges, slides held in mortises in the side walls of the cartridge groove, a lever pivoted to the plate and connected with the slides and reciprocated by the revolution of the gun when in action, substantially as specified.

RICHARD J. GATLING.

Witnesses:
　　HARRY R. WILLIAMS,
　　CLARENCE E. BUCKLAND.

R. J. GATLING.
FEED FOR MAGAZINE GUNS.

No. 502,882.   Patented Aug. 8, 1893.

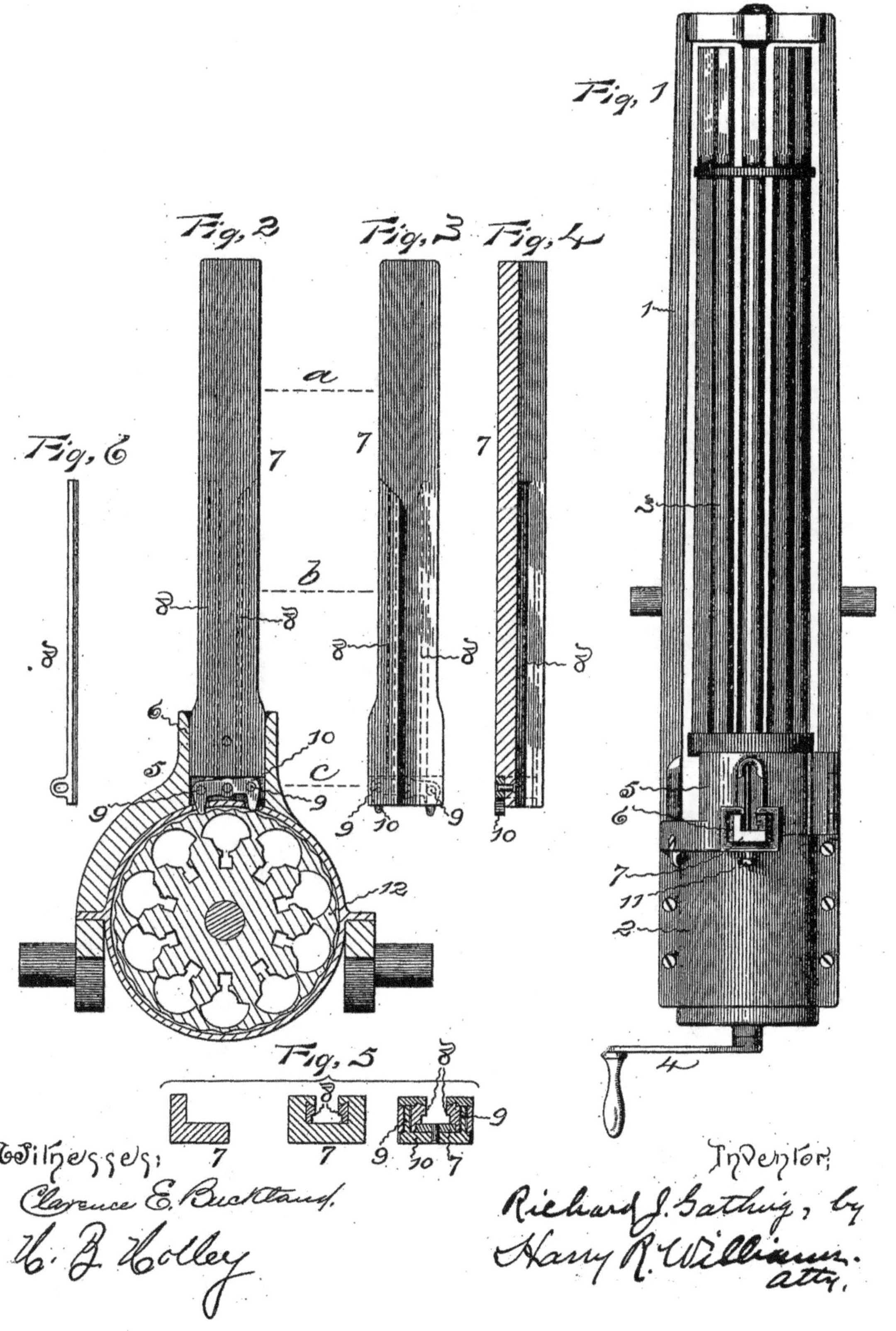

Witnesses:
Clarence E. Buckland.
H. B. Holley

Inventor:
Richard J. Gatling, by
Harry R. Williams,
atty.

UNITED STATES PATENT OFFICE.

RICHARD J. GATLING, OF HARTFORD, CONNECTICUT.

MACHINE-GUN.

SPECIFICATION forming part of Letters Patent No. 504,831, dated September 12, 1893.

Application filed October 20, 1892. Serial No. 449,428. (No model.)

To all whom it may concern:

Be it known that I, RICHARD J. GATLING, a citizen of the United States, residing at Hartford, in the county of Hartford and State of
5 Connecticut, have invented certain new and useful Improvements in Machine-Guns, of which the following is a full, clear, and exact specification.

The invention relates to the class of guns
10 commonly known as Gatling guns, and the object is to so construct such a gun with an infallible feed and stripping mechanism that cartridges may be fed positively and accurately to the revolving carrier in front of the
15 reciprocating locks, by a flexible belt, and one cartridge be surely stripped from the belt and enter each space behind the breech of each barrel when the gun is in action, regardless of the speed of revolution of the carrier.

20 To this end the invention resides in a gun of this class having a revolving group of barrels and lock-carrier-cylinder with reciprocating locks, a hopper with an opening for the passage of the belt and cartridges, arms
25 for stripping the cartridges from the belt, and fingers projecting from the carrier for positively feeding the belt through the hopper, as more particularly hereinafter described and pointed out in the claims.

30 Referring to the accompanying drawings: Figure 1 is a plan view of the gun provided with the improvements. Fig. 2 is an enlarged plan of the hopper. Fig. 3 is a transverse section of the gun on plane denoted by the
35 broken line *a—a*. Fig. 4 is a side view of the hopper. Fig. 5 is a plan of the hopper with the cover removed; and Fig. 6 is a detail view of a portion of the belt with cartridges.

In the views 1 indicates the frame of a Gat-
40 ling gun of ordinary form and construction, having the usual breech-casing 2, group of rotary barrels 3, and crank 4 for revolving the barrels, while at the rear of the barrels just forward of the breech-casing is the hopper 5,
45 which being hinged to one side of the frame and provided with a catch 6 at the other side, may be lifted to uncover the breech of the barrels, as in the common Gatling gun. The hopper 5, which on one side has a shelf 7 for
50 holding the cartridge packages, is cut away on top, and near the opening thus formed by means of a pivot 8, is hinged cover 9 having a catch 10 on the side opposite the hinge to hold it closed over the opening.

The belt 11 has on one surface along each 55 side of the center, at proper intervals, curved spring fingers 12 adapted to clasp and yieldingly hold the cartridges, while between these fingers are downwardly projecting prongs 13.

The cover 9 has a flaring mouth 14 opening 60 toward the shelf 7, and the hopper on that side is cut away enough to permit cartridges to enter the gun through that opening as they are drawn along by the belt, while on the other side the cover closes down nearly to the 65 hopper leaving but a narrow mortise 15 for the passage of the belt. The upper face of the hopper on the hinge side adjacent to the narrow mortise is provided with grooves 16 to permit the passage of the projecting prongs 70 and the fingers that hold the cartridges, but not for the passage of cartridges, the under face of the hopper on this side being so wedge-shaped that the cartridges are stripped from the fingers of the belt and allowed to drop 75 into the carrier as the belt is drawn along.

To the carrier, near the edge of the grooves in which the locks reciprocate in the common Gatling gun, are secured arms 17 that project toward the plane of the center of the belt in 80 such manner that each sweeps around when the gun is in action so as to come in contact with a prong projecting from the belt and pull the belt forward a distance sufficient to enable the wedges on the interior face of the 85 hopper to strip one cartridge from the grasp of the fingers on the belt and bring another prong into the path of the following arm.

The hopper is provided with the customary plows for ejecting the exploded shells, as in 90 the common Gatling gun.

In order to start the feeding of cartridges into the gun the cover of the hopper is raised and the belt laid in the mortise 15 with the first prong in its groove in front of the arm 95 projecting from the top of the carrier, so that when the carrier revolves in action the belt is drawn along an absolute and positive distance each time to enable one cartridge and but one cartridge to be dropped into each carrier 100 groove as it comes around, thus insuring an absolute certainty of feeding a cartridge at the proper time, in order that one will be fired from each barrel every revolution.

Belts holding the cartridges are packed in boxes in any suitable manner so that when put upon the shelf with the box covers removed they may be freely drawn into the gun. The ends of the belts which are preferably provided with fastening buttons and holes are left projecting from the box so that when one belt is nearly run out another may be attached in order to keep up a continuous and rapid feed.

If desired the shelf on the side of the hopper may be made detachable or so as to swing out of the way when not in use holding a box of cartridges, which of course could be held in the hand while the belt is running out.

I claim as my invention—

1. In combination with the revolving barrels of a Gatling gun, a carrier cylinder having projecting arms revolving with the barrels, a hopper hinged to the frame of the gun with an opening for the passage of a belt through it above the carrier in the plane of the projecting arms, and a belt with spring fingers for grasping cartridges and with prongs between each set of fingers projecting into the path of and engaging with the arms on the carrier, adapted to pass through the hopper, substantially as specified.

2. In combination with the revolving barrels of a Gatling gun, a carrier cylinder having projecting arms revolving with the barrels, a hopper hinged to the frame of the gun with an opening for the passage of a belt through it above the carrier, a cover with its bottom face cut away to leave a space for the passage of the belt hinged to the hopper over the opening, a belt with spring fingers for grasping cartridges and with prongs between each set of fingers projecting into the path of and engaging with the arms on the carrier, adapted to pass through the hopper, substantially as specified.

3. In combination with the revolving barrels of a Gatling gun, a carrier cylinder having projecting arms revolving with the barrels, a hopper hinged to the frame of the gun with a wide opening on one side for the entrance of the cartridges and belt and a narrow opening on the opposite side for the passage of the belt only, above the carrier, with grooves through the hopper adjacent to the narrow opening for the passage of the spring fingers and prongs, and a belt with spring fingers for grasping cartridges and with prongs between each set of fingers projecting into the path of and engaging with the arms on the carrier, adapted to pass through the hopper, substantially as specified.

4. In combination with the revolving barrels of a Gatling gun, a carrier cylinder with projecting arms revolving with the barrels, a hopper hinged to the frame of the gun with a wide opening on one side for the entrance of the cartridges and belt and a narrow opening on the opposite side for the passage of the belt only, above the carrier, with grooves through the hopper adjacent to the narrow opening for the passage of the spring fingers and prongs, a cover hinged to the hopper over the opening, with its bottom face cut away to leave a space for the passage of the belt, and a belt with spring fingers for grasping cartridges and with prongs between each set of fingers projecting into the path of and engaging with the arms on the carrier, adapted to pass through the hopper, substantially as specified.

RICHARD J. GATLING.

Witnesses:
CLARENCE E. BUCKLAND,
H. R. WILLIAMS.

R. J. GATLING.
MACHINE GUN.

No. 504,831.   Patented Sept. 12, 1893.

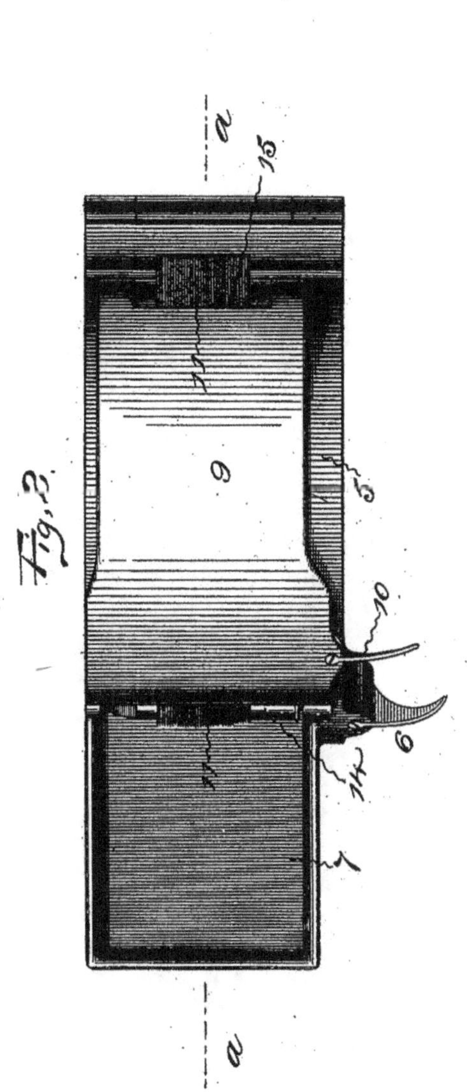

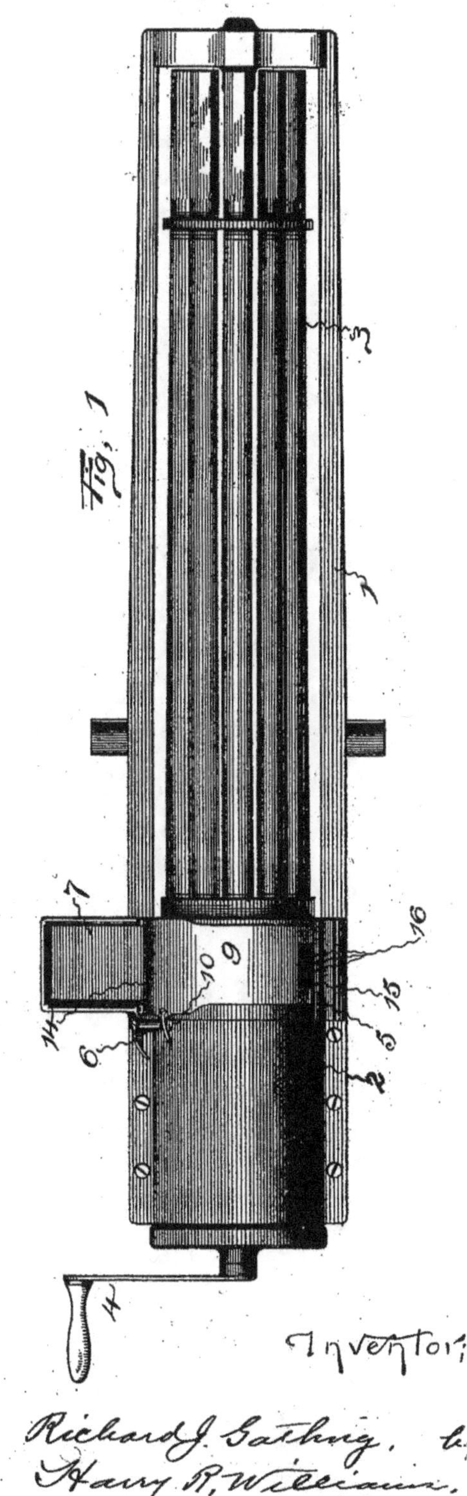

Witnesses:
Clarence E. Buckland.
P. A. Phelps.

Inventor:
Richard J. Gatling, by
Harry R. Williams,
Atty.

R. J. GATLING.
MACHINE GUN.

No. 504,831.   Patented Sept. 12, 1893.

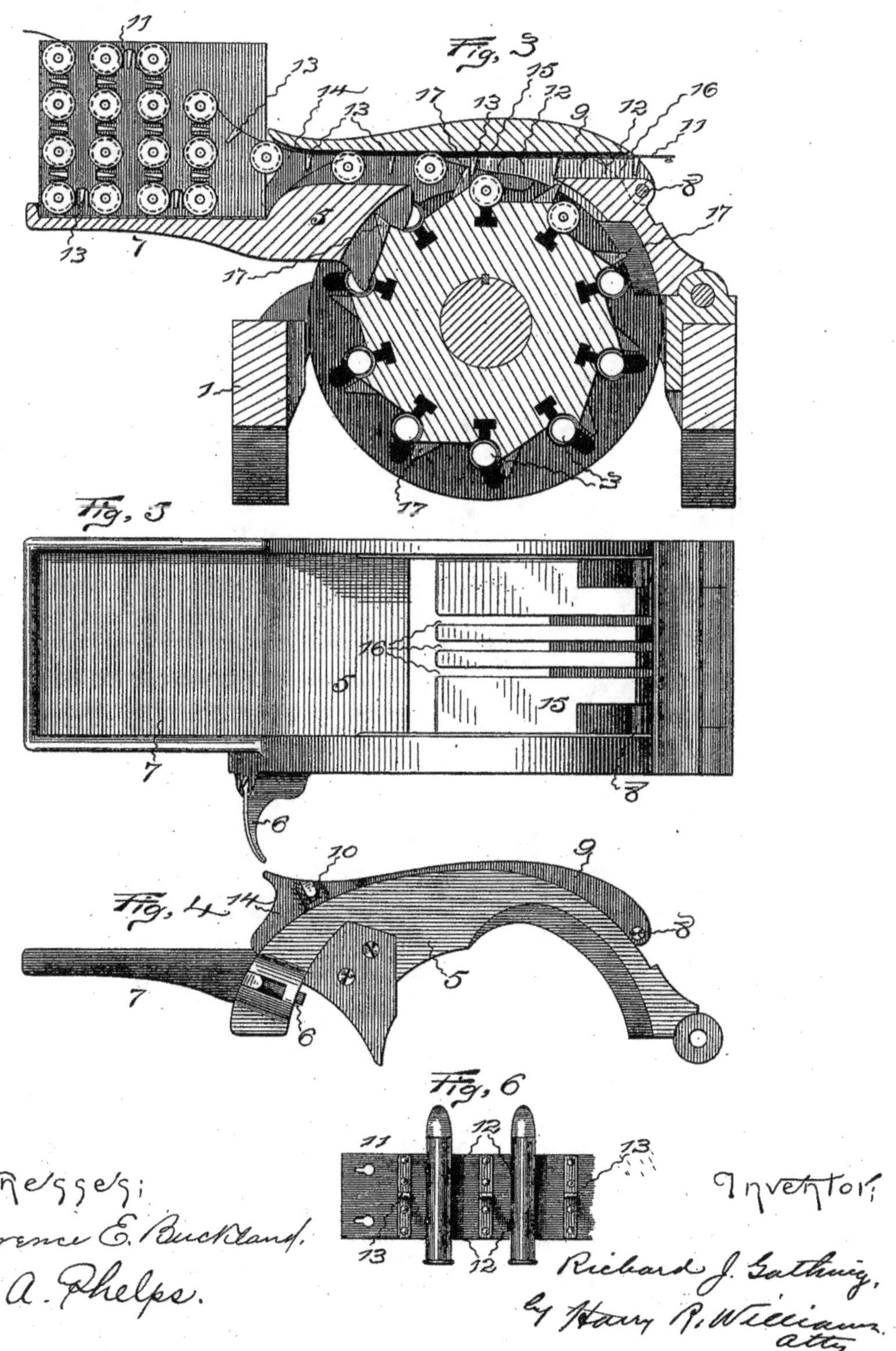

Witnesses:
Clarence E. Buckland.
P. A. Phelps.

Inventor:
Richard J. Gatling,
by Henry R. Williams
atty,